DEFENSE, SECURITY AND STRATEGIES

BEHAVIOR DETECTION ACTIVITIES TO IDENTIFY AVIATION SECURITY THREATS

ASSESSMENTS

DEFENSE, SECURITY AND STRATEGIES

Additional books in this series can be found on Nova's website under the Series tab.

Additional e-books in this series can be found on Nova's website under the e-book tab.

DEFENSE, SECURITY AND STRATEGIES

BEHAVIOR DETECTION ACTIVITIES TO IDENTIFY AVIATION SECURITY THREATS

ASSESSMENTS

RONALD D. FIGUEROA
EDITOR

nova publishers
New York

Library of Congress Cataloging-in-Publication Data

ISBN: 978-1-63117-036-2

Published by Nova Science Publishers, Inc. † New York

CONTENTS

Preface		**vii**
Chapter 1	Aviation Security: TSA Should Limit Future Funding for Behavior Detection Activities *United States Government Accountability Office*	**1**
Chapter 2	Transportation Security Administration's Screening of Passengers by Observation Techniques *Department of Homeland Security, Office of Inspector General*	**87**
Chapter 3	Statement of John S. Pistole, Administrator, Transportation Security Administration. Hearing on "TSA's SPOT Program and Initial Lessons From the LAX Shooting"	**111**
Chapter 4	Statement of Charles K. Edwards, Deputy Inspector General, U.S. Department of Homeland Security. Hearing on "TSA's SPOT Program and Initial Lessons from the LAX Shooting"	**119**
Index		**127**

PREFACE

Available evidence does not support whether behavioral indicators, which are used in the Transportation Security Administration's (TSA) Screening of Passengers by Observation Techniques (SPOT) program, can be used to identify persons who may pose a risk to aviation security. This book addresses the extent to which available evidence supports the use of behavioral indicators to identify aviation security threats, and TSA has the data necessary to assess the SPOT program's effectiveness.

Chapter 1 – TSA began deploying the SPOT program in fiscal year 2007—and has since spent about $900 million—to identify persons who may pose a risk to aviation security through the observation of behavioral indicators. In May 2010, GAO concluded, among other things, that TSA deployed SPOT without validating its scientific basis and SPOT lacked performance measures. GAO was asked to update its assessment. This chapter addresses the extent to which (1) available evidence supports the use of behavioral indicators to identify aviation security threats and (2) TSA has the data necessary to assess the SPOT program's effectiveness. GAO analyzed fiscal year 2011 and 2012 SPOT program data. GAO visited four SPOT airports, chosen on the basis of size, among other things, and interviewed TSA officials and a nonprobability sample of 25 randomly selected BDOs. These results are not generalizable, but provided insights.

Chapter 2 – The authors audited the Transportation Security Administration's (TSA) Screening of Passengers by Observation Techniques program. The program's intent is to screen passengers by observing their behavior in order to detect potential high-risk travelers. This program uses Behavior Detection Officers to detect passenger behaviors that may be indicative of stress, fear, or deception. Congressman Bennie Thompson requested an audit of TSA's Screening of Passengers by Observation Techniques program to determine its effectiveness, efficiency, and economy as a security screening protocol at airports. The audit objective was to determine whether TSA's Screening of Passengers by Observation Techniques program is structured to ensure that passengers at U.S. airports are screened in an objective and cost-effective manner to identify potential terrorists.

Since the Screening of Passengers by Observation Techniques program began in fiscal year 2007, data provided by TSA indicate that the program has expended an estimated $878 million and has more than 2,800 full-time equivalent positions, as of September 30, 2012. However, TSA has not implemented a strategic plan to ensure the program's success. For example, TSA did not (1) assess the effectiveness of the Screening of Passengers by Observation Techniques program, (2) have a comprehensive training program, (3) ensure outreach to its partners, or (4) have a financial plan. As a result, TSA cannot ensure that passengers at United States airports are screened objectively, show that the program is cost-effective, or reasonably justify the program's expansion. In fiscal year 2012, TSA's Behavior Detection and Analysis Division developed a draft strategic plan that includes a statement of mission, goals, and objectives. However, the plan had not been approved and implemented at the time of the authors' review.

The authors made six recommendations to improve the effectiveness of the Screening of Passengers by Observation Techniques program. TSA concurred with all recommendations.

Chapter 3 – Statement of John S. Pistole, Administrator, Transportation Security Administration.

Chapter 4 – Statement of Charles K. Edwards, Deputy Inspector General, U.S. Department of Homeland Security.

In: Behavior Detection Activities ... ISBN: 978-1-63117-036-2
Editor: Ronald D. Figueroa

Chapter 1

AVIATION SECURITY: TSA SHOULD LIMIT FUTURE FUNDING FOR BEHAVIOR DETECTION ACTIVITIES*

United States Government Accountability Office

WHY GAO DID THIS STUDY

TSA began deploying the SPOT program in fiscal year 2007—and has since spent about $900 million—to identify persons who may pose a risk to aviation security through the observation of behavioral indicators. In May 2010, GAO concluded, among other things, that TSA deployed SPOT without validating its scientific basis and SPOT lacked performance measures. GAO was asked to update its assessment. This chapter addresses the extent to which (1) available evidence supports the use of behavioral indicators to identify aviation security threats and (2) TSA has the data necessary to assess the SPOT program's effectiveness. GAO analyzed fiscal year 2011 and 2012 SPOT program data. GAO visited four SPOT airports, chosen on the basis of size, among other things, and interviewed TSA officials and a nonprobability sample of 25 randomly selected BDOs. These results are not generalizable, but provided insights.

---

* This is an edited, reformatted and augmented version of United States Government Accountability Office Publication No. GAO-14-159, dated November 2013.

What GAO Recommends

Congress should consider the absence of scientifically validated evidence for using behavioral indicators to identify threats to aviation security when assessing the potential benefits and cost in making future funding decisions for aviation security. GAO included this matter because DHS did not concur with GAO's recommendation that TSA limit future funding for these activities until it can provide such evidence, in part because DHS disagreed with GAO's analysis of indicators. GAO continues to believe the chapter findings and recommendation are valid.

What GAO Found

Available evidence does not support whether behavioral indicators, which are used in the Transportation Security Administration's (TSA) Screening of Passengers by Observation Techniques (SPOT) program, can be used to identify persons who may pose a risk to aviation security. GAO reviewed four meta-analyses (reviews that analyze other studies and synthesize their findings) that included over 400 studies from the past 60 years and found that the human ability to accurately identify deceptive behavior based on behavioral indicators is the same as or slightly better than chance. Further, the Department of Homeland Security's (DHS) April 2011 study conducted to validate SPOT's behavioral indicators did not demonstrate their effectiveness because of study limitations, including the use of unreliable data. Twenty-one of the 25 behavior detection officers (BDO) GAO interviewed at four airports said that some behavioral indicators are subjective. TSA officials agree, and said they are working to better define them. GAO analyzed data from fiscal years 2011 and 2012 on the rates at which BDOs referred passengers for additional screening based on behavioral indicators and found that BDOs' referral rates varied significantly across airports, raising questions about the use of behavioral indicators by BDOs. To help ensure consistency, TSA officials said they deployed teams nationally to verify compliance with SPOT procedures in August 2013. However, these teams are not designed to help ensure BDOs consistently interpret SPOT indicators.

TSA has limited information to evaluate SPOT's effectiveness, but plans to collect additional performance data. The April 2011 study found that SPOT was more likely to correctly identify outcomes representing a high-risk passenger— such as possession of a fraudulent document—than through a random selection process. However, the study results are inconclusive because of limitations in the design and data collection and cannot be used to demonstrate the effectiveness of SPOT. For example, TSA collected the study data unevenly. In December 2009, TSA began collecting data from 24 airports, added 1 airport after 3 months, and an additional 18 airports more than 7 months later when it determined that the airports were not collecting enough data to reach the study's required sample size. Since aviation activity and passenger demographics are not constant throughout the year, this uneven data collection may have conflated the effect of random versus SPOT selection methods. Further, BDOs knew if passengers they screened were selected using the random selection protocol or SPOT procedures, a fact that may have introduced bias into the study. TSA completed a performance metrics plan in November 2012 that details the performance measures required for TSA to determine whether its behavior detection activities are effective, as GAO recommended in May 2010. However, the plan notes that it will be 3 years before TSA can begin to report on the effectiveness of its behavior detection activities. Until TSA can provide scientifically validated evidence demonstrating that behavioral indicators can be used to identify passengers who may pose a threat to aviation security, the agency risks funding activities that have not been determined to be effective. This is a public version of a sensitive report that GAO issued in November 2013. Information that TSA deemed sensitive has been redacted.

ABBREVIATIONS

ASAP	Aviation Security Assessment Program
BAC	behavior analysis capability
BDA	Behavior Detection and Analysis program
BDAD	Behavior Detection and Analysis Division
BDO	behavior detection officer
BEAM	BDO Efficiency and Accountability Metrics
DHS	Department of Homeland Security
DOJ	Department of Justice
EEO	Equal Employment Opportunity
FAMS	Federal Air Marshal Service
FBI	Federal Bureau of Investigation
FTE	full-time equivalent

JKT	Job Knowledge Test
LEO	law enforcement officer
OIG	DHS Office of Inspector General
OMB	Office of Management and Budget
OOI	Office of Inspection
PASS	Performance Accountability and Standards System
PCA	Performance Compliance Assessment
PC&B	Personnel Compensation and Benefits
PPA	program, project, activity
S&T	Science and Technology Directorate
SPOT	Screening of Passengers by Observation Techniques
TAC	Technical Advisory Committee
TISS	Transportation Information Sharing System
TSA	Transportation Security Administration
TSO	transportation security officer
TSSRA	Transportation Security System Risk Assessment

November 8, 2013

Congressional Requesters

The Department of Homeland Security's (DHS) Transportation Security Administration (TSA) fiscal year 2014 budget request amounts to approximately $7.4 billion for programs and activities to secure the nation's transportation systems. This amount includes nearly $5 billion for TSA's Aviation Security account, a portion of which is requested to support Screening of Passengers by Observation Techniques (SPOT) within the Behavior Detection and Analysis (BDA) program, which seeks to identify persons who may pose a risk to aviation security.[1] Through the SPOT program, TSA's behavior detection officers (BDO) are to identify passenger behaviors indicative of stress, fear, or deception and refer passengers meeting certain criteria for additional screening of their persons and carry-on baggage.[2] During this SPOT referral screening, if passengers exhibit additional behaviors, or if other events occur, such as the discovery of a suspected fraudulent document, BDOs are to refer these passengers to a law enforcement officer (LEO) for further investigation, which could result in an arrest, among other outcomes.

In October 2003, TSA began testing its primary behavior detection activity, the SPOT program, and during fiscal year 2007, TSA deployed the program to 42 TSA-regulated airports.[3] By fiscal year 2012, about 3,000 BDOs were deployed to 176 of the more than 450 TSA-regulated airports in the United States. From fiscal years 2011 through 2012, an estimated 1.3 billion people passed through checkpoints at the 176 SPOT airports. TSA has expended approximately $200 million annually for the SPOT program since fiscal year 2010, and a total of approximately $900 million since 2007. BDOs represent one of TSA's layers of security. In addition to BDOs, other layers of security include travel document checkers, who examine tickets, passports, and other forms of identification; transportation security officers (TSO), who are responsible for screening passengers and their carry-on baggage at passenger checkpoints using X-ray equipment, magnetometers, advanced imaging technology, and other devices; as well as for screening checked baggage; and random employee screening, among others.[4]

In May 2010, we concluded on the basis of our work, among other things, that TSA deployed SPOT nationwide without first validating the scientific basis for identifying passengers who may pose a threat in an airport environment.[5] TSA piloted the SPOT program in 2003 and 2004 at several New England airports. However, the pilot was not designed to determine the effectiveness of using behavior detection techniques to enhance aviation security; rather, the pilot was focused on the operational feasibility of implementing the SPOT program at airports. In recognition of the need to conduct additional research, DHS's Science and Technology Directorate (S&T) hired a contractor in 2007 to design and execute a validation study to determine whether the primary screening instrument used in the program—the SPOT referral report and its associated indicators based on behavior or appearance factors—could be used to correctly identify high-risk passengers. The validation study, published in April 2011, found that the SPOT program identified substantially more "high-risk" passengers—defined by the study as those passengers who, for example, possessed fraudulent documents—as compared with passengers who had been selected by BDOs according to a random selection protocol.[6] However, the validation study cited certain methodological limitations, such as the potential for selection bias as a result of BDOs participating in the study not following the random selection protocols, among others. S&T concluded that the limitations were minimal and that the results were reasonable and reliable. In May 2010, we recommended that S&T convene an independent panel of experts to comment on and evaluate the methodology of the ongoing validation study. In response, S&T established a Technical Advisory Committee (TAC) of 12 researchers and issued a separate report in June 2011 summarizing TAC members' recommendations and opinions on the study results.[7] The results of the validation study and TAC's comments and concerns are discussed later in this chapter.

We also concluded in May 2010 that TSA was experiencing challenges in implementing the SPOT program at airports, such as not systematically collecting and analyzing potentially useful passenger information obtained by BDOs, and that the program lacked outcome-based performance measures useful for assessing the program's effectiveness.[8] As a result, we recommended that TSA take several actions to help assess SPOT's contribution to improving aviation security.[9] Overall, TSA has taken action on all of the 11 recommendations we made, and, as of October 2013, has implemented 10 of the recommendations. For example, among other things, TSA revised SPOT standard operating procedures to more clearly instruct BDOs and other TSA personnel regarding how and when to enter SPOT referral data into the Transportation Information Sharing System (TISS).[10] This would help enable the referral data to be shared with federal, state, or local law enforcement entities. Further, in November 2012, TSA issued a plan to develop outcome-based performance measures, such as the ability of BDOs to consistently identify SPOT behavioral indicators, within 3 years to assess the effectiveness of the SPOT program. This plan is discussed in more detail later in this chapter.

You requested an updated assessment of the SPOT program's effectiveness. Specifically, this chapter addresses the following questions:

1) To what extent does available evidence support the use of behavioral indicators to identify aviation security threats?
2) To what extent does TSA have data necessary to assess the effectiveness of the SPOT program in identifying threats to aviation security?

In addition, we also reviewed information related to recent allegations of profiling in the SPOT program. This information can be found in appendix I.

To address the first question, we reviewed academic and government research on behavior-based deception detection, which we identified through a structured literature search and recommendations from experts in the field. We assessed the reliability of this research against established practices for study design, and through interviews with nine experts we selected based on their published peer-reviewed research in this area.[11] While the results of these interviews cannot be used to generalize about all research on behavior detection, they represent a mix of views and subject matter expertise. We determined that the research was sufficiently reliable for describing the evidence that existed regarding the use of behavioral indicators to identify security threats. We also analyzed documentation related to the April 2011 SPOT validation study, including study protocols and the final reports, and assessed the study against established practices for evaluation design and generally accepted statistical principles.[12] We interviewed headquarters TSA and S&T officials responsible for the validation study and contractor officials. We obtained the data that were used by these officials to reach the conclusions in the validation study. To assess the soundness of the methodology and conclusions in the validation study, we replicated some of the analyses that were conducted by the contractor, based on the methodology described in the final report. Generally, we replicated the study's results, and as an extra step, we extended the analyses using the full sample of SPOT referrals to increase the power to detect significant associations, as described in appendix II. We also analyzed data on BDOs' SPOT referrals, hours worked, and characteristics, such as race and gender, from the SPOT program database, TISS, TSA's Office of Human Capital, and the National Finance Center for fiscal years 2011 and 2012 to determine the extent to which SPOT referrals varied across airports and across BDOs with different characteristics. To assess the reliability of these data, we reviewed relevant documentation, including DHS privacy impact assessments and a 2012 data audit of the SPOT database, and interviewed TSA officials about the controls in place to maintain the integrity of the data.[13] We determined that the data were sufficiently reliable for us to use to standardize the referral data across airports based on the number of hours each BDO spent performing operational SPOT activities.[14] In addition, we interviewed BDA program managers at headquarters, and visited four airports where the SPOT program was implemented in fiscal years 2011 and 2012, and where the validation study was carried out. We selected the airports based on their size, risk ranking, and participation in behavior detection programs.[15] As part of our visits, we interviewed 25 randomly selected BDOs, as well as BDO managers and officials from the responsible local law enforcement agency for each airport.[16] While the results of these visits and interviews are not generalizable to all SPOT airports or BDOs, they provided additional BDO perspectives and helped corroborate the research and statistical information we gathered through other means.

To address the second question, we analyzed documentation related to the April 2011 validation study, including study protocols and the final reports, and evaluated these efforts against established practices for designing evaluations and generally accepted statistical principles.[17] We also reviewed financial data from fiscal years 2007 through 2012 to determine the expenditures associated with the SPOT program, and interviewed officials in DHS's Office of the Inspector General (OIG) who were working on a related audit of the SPOT program.[18] We also reviewed documentation associated with program oversight, including a November 2012 performance metrics plan and evaluated TSA's efforts to collect and analyze data to provide oversight of BDA activities against criteria outlined in Office of Management and Budget guidance, federal government efficiency initiatives, and *Standards for Internal Control in the Federal Government*.[19] Finally, to demonstrate effectiveness of the BDA program, including SPOT, we analyzed documentation such as a returnon-investment analysis and a risk-based allocation analysis, both from December 2012. We interviewed headquarters TSA and S&T officials responsible for the validation study and TSA field officials responsible for collecting study data at the four airports we visited, as well as contractor officials, and 8 of the 12 TAC members.[20] We interviewed BDA officials in the Offices of Security Capabilities and Security Operations, and TSA officials in the Office of Human Capital on the extent to which they collect and analyze data. In addition, to identify additional information about recent allegations of passenger profiling in the SPOT program, we reviewed documentation and data, and interviewed a nongeneralizable sample of 25 randomly selected BDOs and an additional 7 BDOs who contacted us directly. We also interviewed TSA headquarters and field officials, such as federal security directors and BDO managers. Appendix III provides additional details on our objectives, scope, and methodology.

This chapter is a public version of the prior sensitive report that we provided to you. DHS and TSA deemed some of the information in the chapter as sensitive security information, which must be protected from public disclosure. Therefore, this chapter omits sensitive information about specific SPOT behavioral indicators, the validation study findings, and the results of our analysis on the extent to which SPOT referrals varied across airports and across BDOs with different characteristics. Although the information provided in this chapter is more limited in scope, it addresses the same questions as the sensitive report. Also, the overall methodology used for both reports is the same.

We conducted this performance audit from April 2012 to November 2013 in accordance with generally accepted government auditing standards. Those standards require that we plan and perform the audit to obtain sufficient, appropriate evidence to provide a reasonable basis for our findings and conclusions based on our audit objectives. We believe the evidence obtained provides a reasonable basis for our findings and conclusions based on our audit objectives.

BACKGROUND

BDA and the SPOT Program

The Aviation and Transportation Security Act established TSA as the federal agency with primary responsibility for securing the nation's civil aviation system, which includes the screening of all passengers and property transported by commercial passenger aircraft.[21] At the more than 450 TSA-regulated airports in the United States, all passengers, their accessible property, and their checked baggage are screened prior to boarding an aircraft or entering the sterile area of an airport pursuant to statutory and regulatory requirements and TSA-established standard operating procedures.[22] BDA, and more specifically, the SPOT program, constitutes one of multiple layers of security implemented within TSAregulated airports.[23] According to TSA's strategic plan and other program guidance for the BDA program released in December 2012, the goal of the agency's behavior detection activities, including the SPOT program, is to identify high-risk passengers based on behavioral indicators that indicate "mal-intent." For example, the strategic plan notes that in concert with other security measures, behavior detection activities "must be dedicated to finding individuals with the intent to do harm, as well as individuals with connections to terrorist networks that may be involved in criminal activity supporting terrorism."

TSA developed its primary behavior detection activity, the SPOT program, in 2003 as an added layer of security to identify potentially high-risk passengers through behavior observation and analysis techniques.[24] The SPOT program's standard operating procedures state that BDOs are to observe and visually assess passengers, primarily at passenger screening checkpoints, and identify those who display clusters of behaviors indicative of stress, fear, or deception. The SPOT procedures list a point system BDOs are to use to identify potentially high-risk passengers on the basis of behavioral and appearance indicators, as compared with baseline conditions where SPOT is being conducted.[25] A team of two BDOs is to observe passengers as they proceed through the screening process.[26] This process is depicted in figure 1.

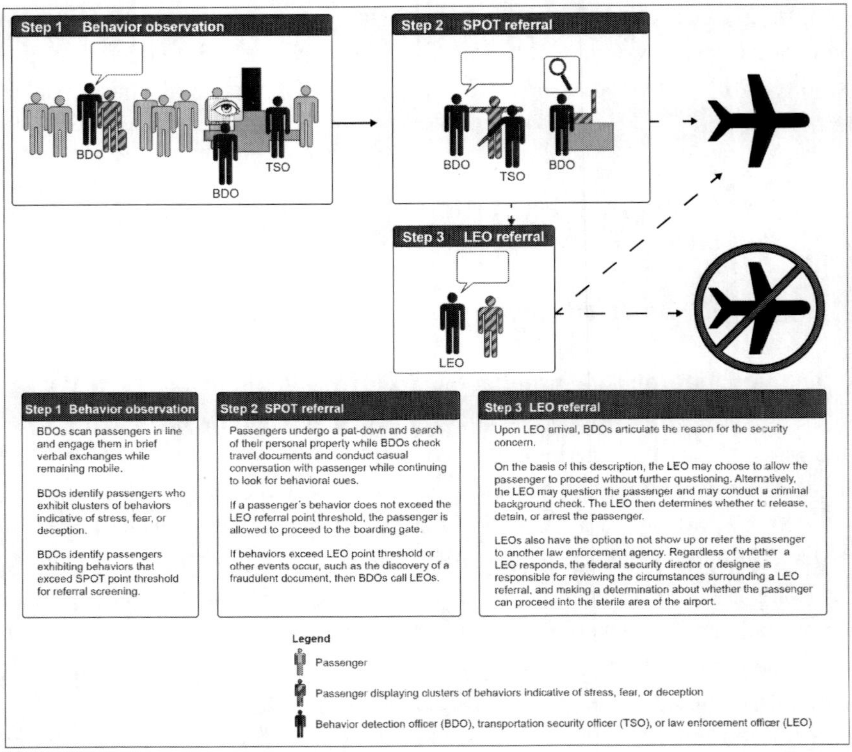

Source: GAO, Art Explosion (clip art).

Figure 1. The Screening of Passengers by Observation Techniques (SPOT) Process.

According to TSA, it takes a BDO less than 30 seconds to meaningfully observe an average passenger.[27] If one or both BDOs observe that a passenger reaches a predetermined point threshold, the BDOs are to direct the passenger and any traveling companions to the second step of the SPOT process—SPOT referral screening. During SPOT referral screening, BDOs are to engage the passenger in casual conversation—a voluntary informal interview—in the checkpoint area or a predetermined operational area in an attempt to determine the reason for the passenger's behaviors and either confirm or dispel the observed behaviors.[28] SPOT referral screening also involves a physical search of the passenger and his or her belongings. According to TSA, an average SPOT referral takes 13 minutes to complete.[29] If the BDOs concur that a passenger's behavior escalates further during the referral screening or if other events occur, such as the discovery of fraudulent identification documents or suspected serious prohibited or illegal items, they are to call a LEO to conduct additional screening—known as a LEO referral— who then may allow the passenger to proceed on the flight, or may question, detain, or arrest the passenger.[30] The federal security director or designee, regardless of whether a LEO responds, is responsible for reviewing the circumstances surrounding a LEO referral and making the determination about whether the passenger can proceed into the sterile area of the airport.

Overview of SPOT Program Funding

The costs of the SPOT program are not broken out as a single line item in the budget. Rather, SPOT program costs are funded through three separate program, project, activity (PPA)-level accounts: (1) BDO payroll costs are funded through the Screener Personnel Compensation and Benefits (PC&B) PPA, (2) the operating expenses of the BDOs and the program are funded through the Screener Training and Other PPA, and (3) the program management payroll costs are funded through the Airport Management and Support PPA. From fiscal year 2007—when the SPOT program began deployment nationwide—through fiscal year 2012, about $900 million has been expended on the program, as shown in figure 2.

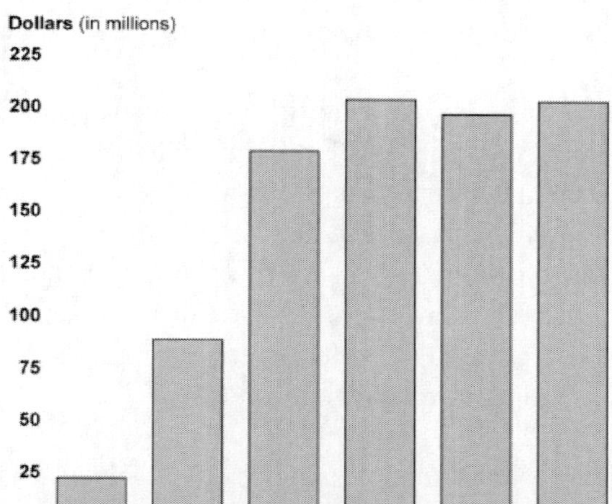

Source: TSA.

Figure 2. TSA Expenditures on the Screening of Passengers by Observation Techniques (SPOT) Program, Fiscal Years 2007 through 2012.

The majority of the funding (approximately 79 percent) for the SPOT program covers workforce costs and is provided under the Screener Personnel Compensation and Benefits PPA. This PPA—for which TSA requested about $3 billion for fiscal year 2014—funds, among other TSA screening activities, BDOs and TSO screening of passengers and their property. The workforce of about 3,000 BDOs is broken into four separate pay bands. The F Band, or Master BDO, and the G Band, or Expert BDO, constitute the primary BDO workforce that screens passengers using behavior detection. The H and I bands are supervisory-level BDOs, responsible for overseeing SPOT operations at the airport level. According to TSA figures, in fiscal year 2012, the average salaries and benefits of an F Band BDO full-time equivalent (FTE) was $66,310; a G Band BDO was $78,162, and the average FTE cost of H and I Band BDO supervisors was $97,392.

Overview of the Validation Study

In 2007, S&T began research to assess the validity of the SPOT program. The contracted study, issued in April 2011, was to examine the extent to which using the SPOT referral report and its indicators, as established in SPOT procedures, led to correct screening decisions at security checkpoints.[31] Two primary studies were designed within the broader validation study:

1) an indicator study: an analysis of the behavioral and appearance indicators recorded in SPOT referral reports over an approximate 5-year period and their relationships to outcomes indicating a possible threat or high-risk passenger, and
2) a comparison study: an analysis over an 11-month period at 43 airports that compared arrests and other outcomes for passengers selected using the SPOT referral report with passengers selected and screened at random, as shown in table 1.[32]

The validation study found, among other things, that some SPOT indicators appeared to be predictors of outcomes indicating a possible threat or high-risk passenger, and that SPOT procedures were more effective than a selection of passengers through a random protocol in identifying outcomes that represent high-risk passengers.

Table 1. Overview of Screening of Passengers by Observation Techniques (SPOT) Validation Study Datasets

	Method of passenger selection	Dates covered	Number of passengers referred for Screening	Number of airports
Indicator study	SPOT procedures	January 1, 2006, through October 31, 2010	247,630	175
Comparison study	Random selection	December 1, 2009, through October 31, 2010	71,589	43
	SPOT procedures	December 1, 2009, through October 31, 2010	23,265	43

Source: DHS validation study.

While the validation study was being finalized, DHS convened a TAC composed of 12 researchers and law enforcement professionals who met for 1 day in February 2011 to evaluate the methodology of the SPOT validation study.[33] According to the TAC report, TAC members received briefings from the contractor that described the study plans and results, but because of TSA's security concerns, TAC members did not receive detailed information about the contents of the SPOT referral report, the individual indicators used in the SPOT program, the validation study data, or the final report containing complete details of the SPOT validation study results. The TAC report noted that several TAC members felt that these restrictions hampered their ability to perform their assigned tasks. According to TSA, TAC members were charged with evaluating the methodology of the study, not the contents of the SPOT referral report. Consequently, TSA officials determined that access to this information was not necessary for the TAC to fulfill its responsibilities. S&T also contracted with another contractor, a human resources research organization, to both participate as TAC members and write a report summarizing the TAC meeting and subsequent discussions among the TAC members. In June 2011, S&T issued the TAC report, which contained TAC recommendations on future work as well as an appendix on TAC dissenting opinions. The findings of the TAC report are discussed later in this chapter.

AVAILABLE EVIDENCE DOES NOT SUPPORT WHETHER BEHAVIORAL INDICATORS CAN BE USED TO IDENTIFY AVIATION SECURITY THREATS

Meta-analyses and other published research studies we reviewed do not support whether nonverbal behavioral indicators can be used to reliably identify deception.[34] While the April 2011 SPOT validation study was a useful initial step and, in part, addressed issues raised in our May 2010 report, it does not demonstrate the effectiveness of the SPOT indicators because of methodological weaknesses in the study. Further, TSA program officials and BDOs we interviewed agree that some of the behavioral indicators used to identify passengers for additional screening are subjective. TSA has plans to study whether behavioral indicators can be reliably interpreted, and variation in referral rates raises questions about the use of the indicators by BDOs.

Published Research Does Not Support Whether the Use of Behavioral Indicators by Human Observers Can Identify Deception

Studies of Nonverbal Indicators to Identify Deception

Peer-reviewed, published research does not support whether the use of nonverbal behavioral indicators by human observers can accurately identify deception.[35] Our review of meta-analyses and other studies related to detecting deception conducted over the past 60 years, and interviews with experts in the field, question the use of behavior observation techniques, that is, human observation unaided by technology, as a means for reliably detecting deception. The meta-analyses, or reviews that synthesize the findings of other studies, we reviewed collectively included research from more than 400 separate studies on detecting deception, and found that the ability of human observers to accurately identify deceptive behavior based on behavioral cues or indicators is the same as or slightly better than chance (54 percent).[36] A 2011 meta-analysis showed weak correlations between most behavioral cues studied and deception. For example, the meta-analysis showed weak correlations for behavioral cues that have been studied the most, such as fidgeting, postural shifts, and lack of eye contact.[37] A 2006 meta-analysis reviewed, in part, the ability of both individuals trained in fields such as law enforcement, as well as those untrained, and found no difference in their ability to detect deception.[38] Additionally, a 2007 meta-analysis on nonverbal indicators of deception states that while there is a general belief that certain nonverbal behaviors are strongly associated with deception—such as an increase in hand, foot, and leg movements—these behaviors are diametrically opposed to observed indicators of deception in experimental studies, which indicate that movements actually decrease when people are lying.[39]

As part of our analysis, we also reviewed scientific research focused on detecting passenger deception in an airport environment. We identified a 2010 study–based on a small sample size of passengers–that reviewed a similar behavior observation program in another country. The first phase of the study found that passengers who were selected based on behaviors were more likely to be referred to airport security officials for further questioning as compared to passengers who had been selected according to a random selection protocol. However, because the physical attributes of the passengers were found to be significantly different between those passengers selected based on behaviors versus those randomly selected, the researchers undertook a second phase of the study to control for those differences. The second phase revealed no differences in initial follow up rate between passengers selected based on behaviors and those matched for physical attributes. That is, when the control group was matched by physical attribute to passengers selected on the basis of behaviors, the follow up rate was the same. The researchers concluded that the higher number of passengers selected based on behaviors and referred for further questioning during the first phase of the study "was more the result of profiling" than the use of behavior observation techniques.[40]

As mentioned earlier in this chapter, the goal of the BDA program is to identify high-risk passengers based on behavioral indicators that may indicate mal-intent. However, other studies we reviewed found that there is little available research regarding the use of behavioral indicators to determine mal-intent, or deception related to an individual's intentions.[41] For example, a 2013 RAND report noted that controversy exists regarding the use of human observation techniques that use behavioral indicators to identify individuals with intent to deceive security officials.[42] In particular, the study noted that while behavioral science has identified nonverbal behaviors associated with emotional and psychological states, these indicators are subject to certain factors, such as individual variability, that limit their potential utility in detecting pre-incident indicators of attack.[43]

The RAND report also found that the techniques for measuring the potential of using behavioral indicators to detect attacks are poorly developed and worthy of further study.[44]

Moreover, a 2008 study performed for the Department of Defense by the JASON Program Office reviewed behavior detection programs, including the methods used by the SPOT program, and found that no compelling evidence exists to support remote observation of physiological signals that may indicate fear or nervousness in an operational scenario by human observers, and no scientific evidence exists to support the use of these signals in detecting or inferring future behavior or intent.[45] In particular, the chapter stated that success in identifying deception and intent in other studies is post hoc and such studies incorrectly equate success in identifying terrorists with the identification of drug smugglers, warrant violators, or others.[46] For example, when describing the techniques used by BDOs in the SPOT program, the chapter concluded that even if a correlation were found between abnormal behaviors and guilt as a result of some transgression, there is no clear indication that the guilt caused the abnormal behavior. The chapter also noted that the determination that the abnormal behavior was caused by guilt was made after the fact, rather than being based on established criteria beforehand.

Studies of Interview Techniques and Automated Technologies to Identify Deception

Recent research on behavior detection has identified more promising results when behavioral indicators are used in combination with certain interview techniques and automated technologies, which are not used as part of the SPOT program. For example, several studies we reviewed that were published in 2012 and 2013 note that specific interviewing techniques, such as asking unanticipated questions, may assist in identifying deceptive individuals.[47] Researchers began to develop automated technologies to detect deception, in part, because humans are limited in their ability to perceive, detect, and analyze all of the potentially useful information about an individual, some of which otherwise would not be noticed by the naked eye.[48] For example, the 2013 RAND report noted that the link between facial microexpressions—involuntary expressions of emotion appearing for milliseconds despite best efforts to dampen or hide them—and deception can be evidenced by coding emotional expressions from a frame-by-frame analysis of video.[49] However, the study concludes that the technique is not suitable for use by humans in real time at checkpoints or other screening areas because of the time lag and hours of labor required for such analysis.[50] Automated technologies are being explored by federal agencies in conjunction with academic researchers to overcome these limitations, as well as human fatigue factors and potential bias in trying to detect deception.[51] Although in the early stages of development, the study stated that automated technologies might be effective at fusing multiple indicators, such as body movement, vocal stress, and facial microexpression analysis.

Methodological Issues Limit the Usefulness of DHS's April 2011 Indicator Validation Study

The usefulness of DHS's April 2011 validation study is limited, in part because the data the study used to examine the extent to which the SPOT behavioral indicators led to correct screening decisions at security checkpoints were from the SPOT database that we had previously found in May 2010 to have several weaknesses, and thus were potentially unreliable.[52] The SPOT indicator study analyzed data collected from 2006 to 2010 to determine the extent to which the indicators could identify high-risk passengers defined as passengers who (1) possessed fraudulent documents, (2) possessed serious prohibited or illegal items, (3) were arrested by a LEO, or (4) any combination of the first three measures.[53] The validation study reported that 14 of the 41 SPOT behavioral indicators were positively and significantly related to one or more of the study outcomes.[54] However, in May 2010, we assessed the reliability of the SPOT database against *Standards for Internal Control in the Federal Government* and concluded that the SPOT database lacked controls to help ensure the completeness and accuracy of the data, such as computerized edit checks to review the format, existence, and reasonableness of data. We found, among other things, that BDOs could not record all behaviors observed in the SPOT database because the database limited entry to eight behaviors, six signs of deception, and four types of serious prohibited items per passenger referred for additional screening. BDOs are trained to identify 94 signs of stress, fear, and deception, or other related indicators.[55] As a result, we determined that, as of May 2010, the data were not reliable enough to conduct a statistical analysis of the association between the indicators and high-risk passenger outcomes. In May 2010, we recommended that TSA make changes to ensure the quality of SPOT referral data, and TSA subsequently made changes to the SPOT database. However, the validation study used data that were collected from 2006 through 2010, prior to TSA's improvements to the SPOT database. Consequently, the data were not sufficiently reliable for use in conducting a statistical analysis of the association between the indicators and high-risk passenger outcomes.

In their report that reviewed the validation study, TAC members expressed some reservations about the methodology used in analyzing the SPOT indicators and suggested that the contractor responsible for completing the study consider not reporting on some of its results and moving the results to an appendix, rather than including them as a featured portion of the chapter.[56] Further, the final validation study report findings were mixed, that is, they both supported and questioned the use of these indicators in the airport environment, and the chapter noted that the study was an "initial step" toward validating the program. However, because the study used unreliable data, its conclusions regarding the use of the SPOT behavioral indicators for passenger screening are questionable and do not support the conclusion that they can or cannot be used to identify threats to aviation security. Other aspects of the validation study are discussed later in this chapter.

Subjective Interpretation of Behavioral Indicators and Variation in Referral Rates Raise Questions about the Use of Indicators; TSA Plans to Study Indicators

BDO Interpretation of Some Behavioral Indicators Is Subjective; TSA Plans Study

BDA officials at headquarters and BDOs we interviewed in four airports said that some of the behavioral indicators are subjective, and TSA has not demonstrated that BDOs can consistently interpret behavioral indicators, though the agency has efforts under way to reduce subjectivity in the interpretation by BDOs. For example, BDA officials at headquarters stated that the definition of some behaviors in SPOT standard operating procedures is subjective. Further, 21 of 25 BDOs we interviewed said that certain behaviors can be interpreted differently by different BDOs. SPOT procedures state that the behaviors should deviate from the environmental baseline. As a result, BDOs' application of the definition of the behavioral indicators may change over time, or in response to external factors.

Four of the 25 BDOs we spoke with said that newer BDOs might be more sensitive in applying the definition of certain behaviors. Our analysis of TSA's SPOT referral data, discussed further below, shows that there is a statistically significant correlation between the length of time that an individual has been a BDO, and the number of SPOT referrals the individual makes per 160 hours worked, or about four 40-hour work weeks. This suggests that different levels of experience may be one reason why BDOs apply the behavioral indicators differently.

BDA officials agree that some of the SPOT indicators are subjective, and the agency is working to better define the behavioral indicators currently used by BDOs. In December 2012, TSA initiated a new contract to review the indicators in an effort to reduce the number of behavioral and appearance indicators used and to reduce subjectivity in the interpretation by BDOs.[57] In June 2013, the contractor produced a document that summarizes information on the SPOT behavioral indicators from the validation study analysis, such as how frequently the indicator was observed, that it says will be used in the indicator review process. According to TSA's November 2012 performance metrics plan, in 2014, the agency also intends to complete an inter-rater reliability study.[58] This study could help TSA determine whether BDOs can reliably interpret the behavioral indicators, which is a critical component of validating the SPOT program's results and ensuring that the program is implemented consistently.

Referral Rates Raise Questions about the Use of Behavioral Indicators

Our analysis of SPOT referral data from fiscal years 2011 and 2012 indicates that SPOT and LEO referral rates vary significantly across BDOs at some airports, which raises questions about the use of behavioral indicators by BDOs.[59] Specifically, we found that variation exists in the SPOT referral rates among 2,199 nonmanager BDOs and across the 49 airports in our review, after standardizing the referral data to take account of the differences in the amount of time each BDO spent observing passengers, as shown in figure 3.[60]

The SPOT referral rates of BDOs ranged from 0 to 26 referrals per 160 hours worked during the 2-year period we reviewed. Similarly, LEO referral rates of BDOs ranged from 0 to 8 per 160 hours worked.[61] Further, at least 153 of the 2,199 nonmanager BDOs were never identified as the primary BDO responsible for a referral. Of these, at least 76 were not associated with a referral during the 2-year period we reviewed.[62]

To better understand the variation in referral rates, we analyzed whether certain variables affected SPOT referral rates and LEO referral rates, including the airport at which the referral occurred, and BDO characteristics, such as their annual performance scores, years of experience, as well as demographic information, including age and gender.[63] The variables we identified as having a statistically significant relationship to the referral rates are shown in table 2.[64]

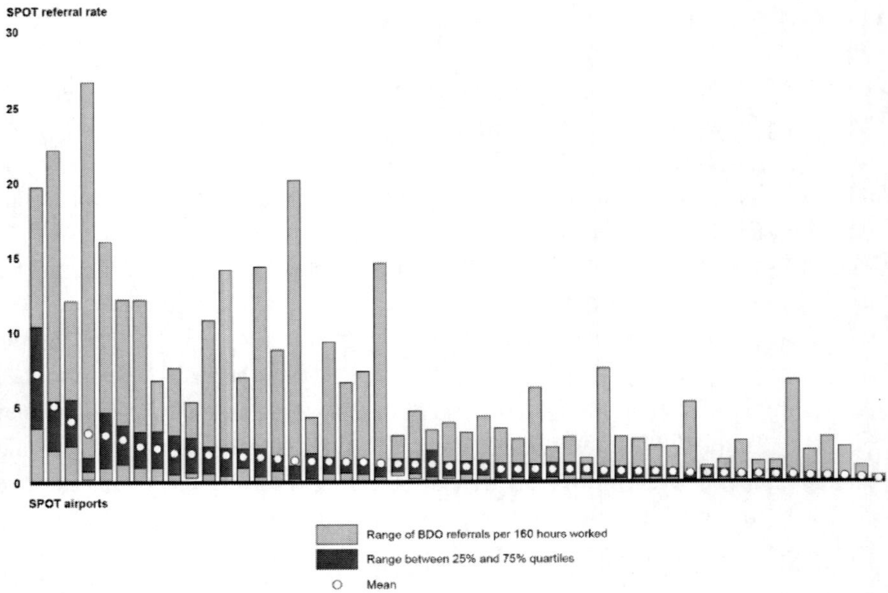

Source: GAO analysis of TSA data.

Notes: Referral rates are calculated per 160 hours worked by 2,199 nonmanager BDOs performing SPOT activities and exclude other BDO time, such as training and leave. For each airport, the mean BDO referral rate is bounded by the total range of values across all BDOs, and the interquartile range, which is the middle 50 percent between the 25th percentile and 75th percentile across all BDOs. More information about this analysis can be found in appendix IV.

[a]Multiple refers to a group of BDOs who made referrals at more than one airport.

Figure 3. Behavior Detection Officer (BDO) Rates for 49 Screening of Passengers by Observation Techniques (SPOT) Airports, Fiscal Years 2011 and 2012.

We found that overall, the greatest amount of the variation in SPOT referral rates by BDOs was explained by the airport in which the referral occurred. That is, a BDO's SPOT referral rate was associated with the airport at which he or she was conducting SPOT activities. However, separate analyses we conducted indicate that these differences across airports were not fully accounted for by another variable that is directly related to individual airports. That variable accounted for less than half of the variation in SPOT referral rates accounted for by airports. Combined, the remaining variables– including BDO performance score, age, years of BDO experience, years of TSA experience, race, and educational level– accounted for little of the variation in SPOT referral rates.

Table 2. Variables Affecting Screening of Passengers by Observation Techniques (SPOT) Referral Rates and Law Enforcement Officer (LEO) Referral Rates at 49 Airports, Fiscal Years 2011 and 2012

	Variables							
	Airport	Behavior detection officer (BDO) performance score[a]	BDO age	Years of BDO experience	Years of Transportation Security Administration (TSA) experience	BDO gender	BDO race	BDO educational level[b]
SPOT referral rate	√	√	—	√	√	—	√	—
LEO referral rate	√	√	√	—	—	√	√	—

In commenting on this issue, TSA officials noted that variation in referral rates across airports could be the result of differences in passenger composition, the airport's market type, the responsiveness of LEOs to BDO referrals, and the number and type of airlines at the airports, among other things. However, because TSA could not provide additional supporting data on these variables with comparable time frames, we were not able to include these variables in our analysis.[65] See appendix IV for a more detailed discussion of the findings from our multivariate analysis of referral rates.

According to TSA, having clearly defined and consistently implemented standard operating procedures for BDOs in the field at the 176 SPOT airports is key to the success of the program. In May 2010, we found that TSA established standardization teams designed to help ensure consistent implementation of the SPOT standard operating procedures.[66] We followed up on TSA's use of standardization teams and found that from 2012 to 2013, TSA made standardization team visits to 9 airports. In May 2012, officials changed their approach and data collection requirements and changed the name of the teams to program compliance assessment teams. From December 2012 through March 2013, TSA conducted pilot site visits to 3 airports to test and refine new compliance team protocols for data collection, which, among other things, involve more quantitative analysis of BDO performance. The pilot process was designed to help ensure that the program compliance assessment teams conduct standardized, on-site evaluations of BDOs' compliance with the SPOT standard operating procedures in a way that is based on current policy and procedures.[67] As of June 2013, TSA had visited and collected data at 6 additional airports and was refining data input and reporting processes. According to BDA officials, TSA deployed the new compliance teams nationally in August 2013 and anticipates visiting an additional 13 airports by the end of fiscal year 2013. However, the compliance teams are not generally designed to help ensure BDOs' ability to consistently interpret the SPOT indicators, and the agency has not developed other mechanisms to measure inter-rater reliability.[68] TSA does not have reasonable assurance that BDOs are reliably interpreting passengers' behaviors within or among airports, in part because of the subjective interpretation of some SPOT behavioral indicators by BDOs and the limited scope of the compliance teams. This, coupled with the inconsistency in referral rates across different airports, raises questions about the use of behavioral indicators to identify potential threats to aviation.

TSA Has Limited Information to Evaluate SPOT Program Effectiveness but Plans to Collect Additional Performance Data

TSA has limited information to evaluate SPOT program effectiveness because the findings from the April 2011 validation comparison study are inconclusive because of methodological weaknesses in the study's overall design and data collection. However, TSA plans to collect additional performance data to help it evaluate the effectiveness of its behavior detection activities.

Methodological Issues Affect the Results of DHS's Study Comparing SPOT with Random Selection of Passengers

Design Limitations

DHS's 2011 validation study compared the effectiveness of SPOT with a random selection of passengers and found that SPOT was between 4 and 52 times more likely to correctly identify a high-risk passenger than random selection, depending on which of the study's outcome measures was used to define persons knowingly and intentionally trying to defeat the security process.[69] However, BDOs used various methods to randomly select passengers during data collection periods of differing length at the study airports. Initially, the contractor proposed that TSA use random selection methods at a sample of 143 SPOT airports, based on factors such as the number of airport passengers.[70] If properly implemented, the proposed sample would have helped ensure that the validation study findings could be generalized to all SPOT airports. However, according to the study and interviews with the contractor, TSA selected a nonprobability sample of 43 airports based on input from local TSA airport officials who decided to participate in the study. TSA allowed the managers of these airports to decide which checkpoints would use random procedures and when they would do so during airport operating hours. According to the validation study and a contractor official, the airports included in the study were not randomly selected because of the increased time and effort it would take to collect study data at the 143 airports proposed by the contractor. Therefore, the study's results may provide insights about the implementation of the SPOT program at the 43 airports where the study was carried out, but they are not generalizable to all 176 SPOT airports.

Additionally, TSA collected the validation study data unevenly and experienced challenges in collecting an adequate sample size for the randomly selected passengers, facts that might have further affected the representativeness of the findings. According to established evaluation design practices, data collection should be sufficiently free of bias or other significant errors that could lead to inaccurate conclusions.[71] Specifically, in December 2009, TSA initially began collecting data from 24 airports whose participation in the study was determined by the local TSA officials. More than 7 months later, TSA added another 18 airports to the study when it determined that enough data were not being collected on the randomly selected passengers at participating airports to reach the study's required sample size.[72] The addition of the airports coincided with a substantial increase in referrals for additional screening and an uneven collection of data, as shown in figure 4.

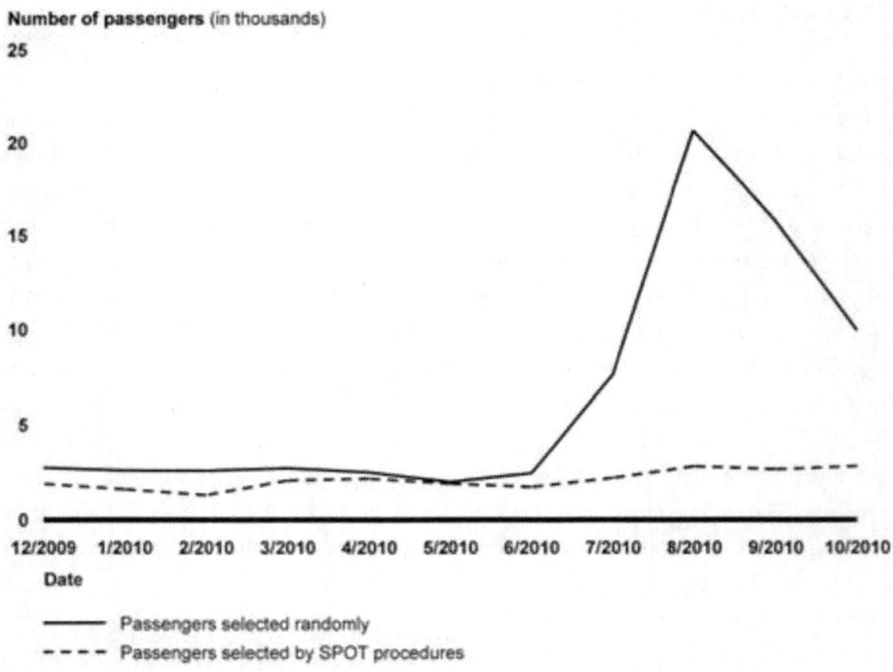

Source: GAO analysis of DHS validation study data.

Figure 4. Comparison Study Data Collected at 43 Airports by Month, December 2009 through October 2010.

As a result of this uneven data collection, study data on 61 percent of randomly selected passengers were collected during the 3-month period from July through September 2010. By comparison, 33 percent of the data on passengers selected by the SPOT program were collected during the same time. Because commercial aviation activity and the demographics of the traveling public are not constant throughout the year, this uneven data collection may have conflated the effect of random versus SPOT selection methods with differences in the rates of high-risk passengers when TSA used either method.

In addition, the April 2011 validation study noted that BDOs were aware of whether the passengers they were screening were selected as a result of the random selection protocol or SPOT procedures, which had the potential to introduce bias in the assessment. According to established practices for evaluation design, when feasible, many scientific studies use "blind" designs, in which study participants do not know which procedures are being evaluated. This helps avoid potential bias due to the tendency of participants to behave or search for evidence in a manner that supports the effects they expect each procedure to have.[73] In contrast, in the SPOT comparison study, BDOs knew whether each passenger they screened was selected through SPOT or random methods. This may have biased BDOs' screening for high-risk passengers, because BDOs could have expected randomly selected passengers to be lower risk and thus made less effort to screen passengers.[74] In interviews, the contractor and four of the eight members of the TAC we interviewed agreed that this may be a design weakness.[75] One TAC member told us that the comparison study would have been more robust if the passengers had been randomly selected by people without any prior knowledge of SPOT indicators to decrease the possibility of bias. To reduce the possibility of bias in the study, another TAC member suggested that instead of using the same BDOs to select and screen passengers, some BDOs could have been responsible for selecting passengers and other BDOs for screening the passengers, regardless of whether they were selected randomly or by SPOT procedures. According to validation study training materials, BDOs were used to select both groups of passengers in an effort to maintain normal security coverage during the study. Another TAC member stated that controls were needed to ensure that BDOs gave the same level of scrutiny to randomly selected passengers as those referred because of their behaviors. The contractor officials reported that they were aware of the potential bias, and tried to mitigate its potential effects by training BDOs who participated in the validation study to screen passengers identically, regardless of how they were selected. However, the contractor stated that they could not fully control these selections because BDOs were expected to conduct their regular SPOT duties concurrently during the study's data collection on random passenger screening.[76] The validation study discussed several limitations that had the potential to introduce bias, but concluded that they did not affect the results of the study.

Our analysis of the validation study data regarding one of the primary high-risk outcome measures—LEO arrests—suggests that the screening process was different for passengers depending on whether they were selected using SPOT procedures or the random selection protocol. Therefore, the study's finding that SPOT was much more likely to identify high-risk passengers who were ultimately arrested by a LEO may be considerably inflated.[77] Specifically, a necessary condition influencing the rate of the arrest outcome measure—exposure to a LEO through a LEO referral—was not equal in the two groups. The difference between the groups occurred because randomly selected passengers were likely to begin the SPOT referral process with zero points or very few points, whereas passengers selected on the basis of SPOT began the process at the higher, established point threshold required for BDOs to make a SPOT referral. However, because the point threshold for a LEO referral was the same for both groups, the likelihood that passengers selected using SPOT would escalate to the next point threshold, resulting in a LEO referral and possible LEO arrest, was greater than for passengers selected randomly. Our analysis showed that because of the discrepancy in the points accrued prior to the start of the referral process, passengers who were selected on the basis of SPOT behavioral indicators were more likely to be referred to a LEO than randomly selected passengers. Our analysis indicates that the validation study design could have been improved by treating each group similarly, regardless of the passengers' accumulated points. For example, as a possible approach, both groups could have been referred to LEOs only in the cases where BDOs discovered a serious prohibited or illegal item. Established study design practices state that identifying key factors known to influence desired evaluation outcomes will aid in forming treatment and comparison groups that are as similar as possible, thus strengthening the analyses' conclusions.[78]

Additionally, once referred to a LEO, passengers selected at random were arrested for different reasons than those selected on the basis of SPOT indicators, which suggests that the two groups of passengers were subjected to different types of screening. All randomly selected passengers who were identified as high risk, referred to a LEO, and ultimately arrested possessed fraudulent documents or serious prohibited or illegal items.[79] In contrast, most of the passengers arrested after having been referred on the basis of SPOT behavior indicators were arrested for reasons other than fraudulent documents or serious prohibited or illegal items. These reasons for arrest included outstanding warrants by law enforcement agencies, public intoxication, suspected illegal entry into the United States, and disorderly conduct.[80]

Such differences in the reasons for arrest suggest that referral screening methods may have varied according to the method of selection for screening, consistent with the concerns of the TAC members and the contractor. Thus, because randomly selected passengers were assigned points differently during screening and consequently referred to LEOs far less than those referred by SPOT, and because being referred to a LEO is a necessary condition for an arrest, the results related to the LEO arrest metric are questionable and cannot be relied upon to demonstrate SPOT program effectiveness.

Monitoring Weaknesses

To help ensure that all of the BDOs carried out the comparison study as intended, protocols for randomly selecting passengers were established that would help ensure that the methods would be the same across airports. The contractor emphasized that deviating from the prescribed protocol could increase the likelihood of introducing systematic differences across airports in the methods of random screening, which could bias the results. To ensure that airports and BDOs followed the study protocols, the contractor conducted monitoring visits at 17 of the 43, or 40 percent, of participating airports. The first monitoring visits occurred 6 months after data collection began, and 9 of the 17 airports were not visited until the last 2 months of the study, as shown in figure 5.[81] Consequently, for 9 of these airports, the contractor could not have addressed the deviations from the protocols that were identified during the data-monitoring visits until the last weeks of data collection.

In the April 2011 report of all 17 monitoring visits that were conducted, the most crucial issue the contractor identified was that BDOs deviated from the random selection protocol in ways that did not meet the criteria for systematic random selection. For example, the contractor found that across airports, local TSA officials had independently decided to exclude certain types of passengers from the study because the airport officials felt it was unreasonable to subject these types of passengers to referral screening. At 1 airport visited less than 4 weeks before data collection ended, BDOs misunderstood the protocols and incorrectly excluded a certain type of passenger.[82] As a result, certain groups of potentially lower-risk passengers were systematically excluded from the population eligible for random selection. In addition, the contractor found that some BDOs used their own methods to select passengers, rather than the random selection protocol that was specified.

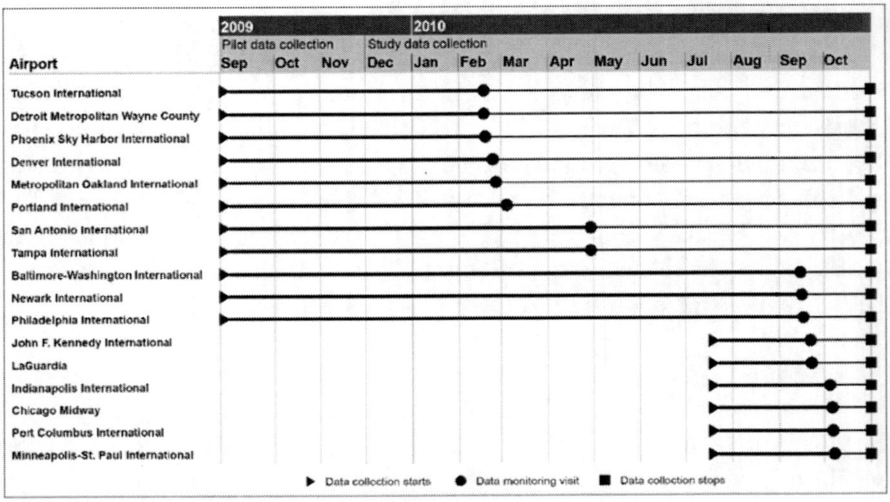

Source: GAO analysis of DHS validation study data.

Note: This represents 17 of the 43 airports in the comparison study in which the contractor conducted data-monitoring visits. The remaining 26 airports collecting data for the study were not visited.

Figure 5. Timeline of Data Monitoring Visits Conducted at 17 Airports for the Comparison Study, September 2009 through October 2010.

The contractor reported that if left uncorrected, this deviation from the protocols could increase the likelihood of introducing systematic bias into the study. For example, at one airport visited less than 6 weeks before data collection ended, BDOs selected passengers by attempting to generate numbers they thought were random by calling out numbers spontaneously, such as "seven," and using the numbers to select the seventh passenger, instead of following the random selection protocol. At another airport visited less than 6 weeks before data collection ended, contrary to random selection protocols, BDOs, rather than the data collection coordinator, selected passengers to undergo referral screening.[83] Although deviations from the protocol may not have produced a biased sample, any deviation from the selection protocol suggests that BDOs' judgment may have affected the random selection and screening processes in the comparison study.

In addition to the limitations cited above, the April 2011 validation study noted other limitations such as the limited data useful for measuring high-risk passenger outcomes, the lack of information on the specific location within the airport where each SPOT indicator was first observed, and difficulties in differentiating whether passengers were referred because of observed behaviors related to elevated indicators of stress, fear, and deception, or for other reasons. The validation study concluded that further research to fully validate and evaluate the SPOT program was warranted. Similarly, the TAC report cited TAC members' concerns that the validation study results "could be easily misinterpreted given the limited scope of the study and the caveats to the data," and that the "results should be presented as a first step in a broader evaluation process." Thus, limitations in the study's design and in monitoring how it was implemented at airports could have affected the accuracy of the study's conclusions, and limited their usefulness in determining the effectiveness of the SPOT program. As a result, the incidence of high-risk passengers in the normal passenger population remains unknown, and the incidence of high-risk passengers identified by random selection cannot be compared with the incidence of those identified using SPOT methods.

TSA Plans to Collect and Analyze Needed Performance Data

TSA plans to collect and analyze additional performance data needed to assess the effectiveness of its behavior detection activities. In response to recommendations we made in May 2010 to conduct a cost-benefit analysis and a risk assessment, TSA completed two analyses of the BDA program in December 2012, but needs to complete additional analysis to fully address our recommendations.[84] Specifically, TSA completed a return-on-investment analysis and a risk-based allocation analysis, both of which were designed in part to inform the future direction of the agency's behavior detection activities, including the SPOT program.[85] The return-on-investment analysis assessed the additional value that BDOs add to TSA's checkpoint screening system, and concluded that BDOs provide an integral value to the checkpoint screening process.[86] However, the chapter did not fully support its assumptions related to the threat frequency or the direct and indirect consequence of a successful attack, as is recommended by best practices.[87] For example, TSA officials told us that the threat and consequence assumptions in the analysis were designed to be consistent with the 2013 Transportation Security System Risk Assessment (TSSRA), but the analysis did not explain why a catastrophic event was the only relevant threat scenario considered when determining consequence.[88] Additionally, the analysis relied on assumptions regarding the effectiveness of BDOs and other countermeasures that were based on questionable information. For example, the analysis relied on results reported in the April 2011 validation study—which, as discussed earlier, had several methodological limitations—as evidence of the effectiveness of BDOs. Further, a May 2013 DHS OIG report found that TSA could not accurately assess the effectiveness or evaluate the progress of the SPOT program because it had not developed a system of performance measures at the time of the OIG review.[89] In response, TSA provided the OIG with a draft version of its performance metrics plan. This plan has since been finalized and is discussed further below.

TSA's risk-based allocation analysis found that an additional 584 BDO FTEs should be allocated to smaller airports in an effort to cover existing gaps in physical screening coverage and performance, an action that, if implemented, would result in an annual budgetary increase of approximately $42 million.[90] One of the primary assumptions in the risk-based allocation analysis is related to the effectiveness of BDOs. For example, this analysis suggests that BDOs may be effective in identifying threats to aviation security where gaps exist in physical screening coverage and performance, including the use of walk-through metal detectors and advanced imaging technology machines. However, TSA has not evaluated the effectiveness of BDOs in comparison with these other screening methods.

In response to an additional recommendation in our May 2010 report to develop a plan for outcome-based performance measures, TSA completed a performance metrics plan in November 2012, which details the performance measures required for TSA to determine whether the agency's behavior detection activities are effective, and identifies the gaps that exist in its current data collection efforts.[91] The plan defined an ideal set of 40 metrics within three major categories that BDA needs to collect to be able to understand and measure the performance of its behavior detection activities. TSA then identified the gaps in its current data collection efforts, such as, under the human factors subcategory, data on BDO fatigue levels and what staffing changes would need to be made to reduce the negative impact on BDO performance resulting from fatigue, as shown in figure 6.

Category	Status	Subcategory	Key gaps[a]
Human capital management	Collecting a low level of data needed for performance management	Operational management	Playbook, checkpoint, and Visible Intermodal Prevention and Response (VIPR)[b] staffing, administrative time
	Not collecting or analyzing	Human factors	Impact of fatigue, optimal duty cycle
Performance	Collecting a low level of data needed for performance management	Individual performance	Inter-rater indicator reliability, tone, questioning techniques and information elicitation skills, customer service, standard operating procedures compliance, behavior detection skills
Security effectiveness	Collecting a low level of data needed for performance management	Probability of detection	Inter-rater indicator reliability, base rate data, behavior detection officer (BDO) value to playbook, BDO value to VIPR
	Not collecting or analyzing	Probability of encounter	Percentage of population meaningfully assessed by BDOs; percentage engaged by BDOs

Legend
- Not collecting or analyzing
- Collecting a low level of data needed for performance management
- Collecting the majority of data needed for performance management
- Collecting all data needed for performance management

Source: TSA's Performance Metrics Plan.

Notes: For example, a low level of data refers to metrics that have been collected only one or two times and have no future scheduled recurrence.

[a]Key gaps refers to program components or performance measures for which TSA does not currently collect the data needed to understand and measure the performance of BDA's activities.

[b]The VIPR Program works with local security and law enforcement officials to conduct a variety of security tactics to introduce unpredictability and deter potential terrorist actions, including random high-visibility patrols at locations other than airports, and includes passenger and baggage screening operations involving BDOs and explosive detection canine teams and technologies.

Figure 6. TSA's Overall Assessment of Behavior Detection and Analysis (BDA) Data Collection Metrics, November 2012.

As of June 2013, TSA had collected some information for 18 of 40 metrics the plan identified.[92] Once collected, the data identified by the plan may help support the completion of a more substantive return-on-investment analysis and risk-based allocation analysis, but according to TSA's November 2012 plan, TSA is currently collecting little to none of the data required to assess the performance and security effectiveness of BDA or the SPOT program. For example, TSA does not currently collect data on the percentage of time a BDO is present at a checkpoint or other areas in the airport while it is open. Without this information, the assumptions contained in TSA's risk-based allocation analysis cannot be validated. This analysis identified the existing BDO coverage level at the airports where SPOT was deployed in 2011, and based its recommendations for an additional 584 BDOs on this coverage level.

In May 2013, TSA began to implement a new data collection system, BDO Efficiency and Accountability Metrics (BEAM), designed to track and analyze BDO daily operational data, including BDO locations and time spent performing different activities. According to BDA officials, this data will allow the agency to gain insight on how BDOs are utilized, and improve analysis of the SPOT program. The performance metrics plan may also provide other useful information in support of some of the other assumptions in TSA's risk-based allocation analysis and return-on investment analysis. For example, both analyses assumed that a BDO can meaningfully assess 450 passengers per hour, and that fatigue would degrade this rate over the course of a day. However, according to the performance metrics plan, TSA does not currently collect any of the information required to assess the number of passengers meaningfully assessed by BDOs, BDOs' level of fatigue, or the impact that fatigue has on their performance.[93] To address these and other deficiencies, the performance metrics plan identifies 22 initiatives that are under way or planned as of November 2012, including efforts discussed earlier in this chapter, such as the indicator study and efforts to improve the SPOT compliance teams, among others. For additional information about the metrics that will result from these initiatives, see appendix V.

These data could help TSA assess the performance and security effectiveness of BDA and the SPOT program, and find ways to become more efficient with fewer resources in order to meet the federal government's long-term fiscal challenges, as recommended by federal government efficiency initiatives.[94] In lieu of these data, TSA uses arrest and LEO referral statistics to help track the program's activities. Of the approximately 61,000 referrals made over the 2-year period at the 49 airports we analyzed, approximately 8,700 (14 percent) resulted in a referral to a LEO.[95] Of these LEO referrals, 365 (4 percent) resulted in an arrest. The proportion of LEO referrals that resulted in an arrest (arrest ratio) could be an indicator of the potential relationship between the SPOT behavioral indicators and an arrest.[96] As shown in figure 7, 99.4 percent of the passengers that were selected for referral screening—that is further questioning and inspection by a BDO—were not arrested. The percentage of passengers referred to LEOs that were arrested was about 4 percent; the other 96 percent of passengers referred to LEOs were not arrested. The SPOT database identifies 6 reasons for arrest, including (1) fraudulent documents, (2) illegal alien, (3) other, (4) outstanding warrants, (5) suspected drugs, and (6) undeclared currency.[97]

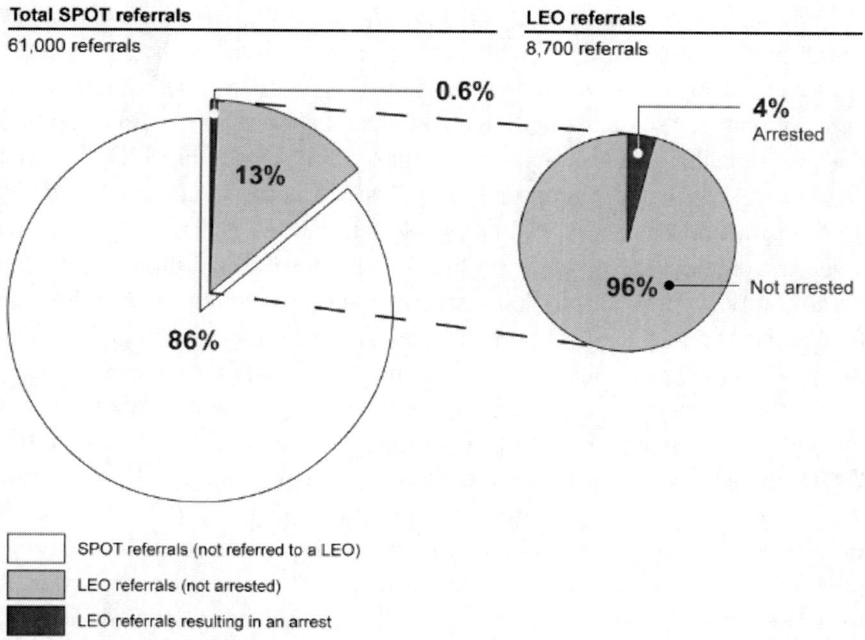

Note: Totals do not add up to 100 percent because of rounding.
Source: GAO analysis of TSA data.

Figure 7. Percentage of Screening of Passengers by Observation Techniques (SPOT) Referrals Resulting in Law Enforcement Officer (LEO) Referrals and Arrests at 49 Airports, Fiscal Years 2011 and 2012.

In February 2013, BDA officials said between 50 and 60 SPOT referrals were forwarded by the Federal Air Marshal Service to other law enforcement agencies for further investigation to identify potential ties to terrorism.[98] For example, TSA provided documentation of three suspicious incident reports from 2011 of passengers who were referred by BDOs to LEOs based on behavioral indicators, and who were later found to be in possession of large sums of U.S. currency.[99] According to a FAMS report on these incident reports, the identification of large amounts of currency leaving the United States could be the first step in the disruption of funding for terrorist organizations or other form of criminal enterprise that may or may not be related to terrorism. TSA officials said it is difficult to identify the terrorism-related nexus in these referrals because they are rarely, if ever, informed on the outcomes of the investigations conducted by other law enforcement agencies, and thus have no way of knowing if these SPOT referrals were ultimately connected to terrorism-related activities or investigations.

Standards for Internal Control in the Federal Government calls for agencies to report on the performance and effectiveness of their programs.[100] However, according to the performance metrics plan, TSA will require at least an additional 3 years and additional resources before it can begin to report on the performance and security effectiveness of BDA or the SPOT program. Given the scope of the proposed activities and some of the challenges that TSA has faced in its earlier efforts to assess the SPOT program at the national level, to complete the activities in the time frames outlined in the plan would be difficult. In particular, the plan notes it is unrealistic that TSA will be able to evaluate the BDO security effectiveness contribution at each airport within the 3-year timeframe. According to best practices for program management of acquisitions, technologies should be demonstrated to work reliably in their intended environment prior to program deployment.[101] Further, according to OMB guidance accompanying the fiscal year 2014 budget, it is incumbent upon agencies to use resources on programs that have been rigorously evaluated and determined to be effective, and to fix or eliminate those programs that have not demonstrated results.[102] TSA has taken a positive step toward determining the effectiveness of BDA's behavior detection activities by developing the performance metrics plan, as we recommended in May 2010. However, 10 years after the development of the SPOT program, TSA cannot demonstrate the effectiveness of its behavior detection activities. Until TSA can provide scientifically validated evidence demonstrating that behavioral indicators can be used to identify passengers who may pose a threat to aviation security, the agency risks funding activities that have not been determined to be effective.

CONCLUSION

TSA has taken several positive steps to validate the scientific basis and strengthen program management of BDA and the SPOT program, which has been in place for over 6 years at a total cost of approximately $900 million since 2007. Nevertheless, TSA has not demonstrated that BDOs can consistently interpret the SPOT behavioral indicators, a fact that may contribute to varying passenger referral rates for additional screening. The subjectivity of the SPOT behavioral indicators and variation in BDO referral rates raise questions about the continued use of behavior indicators for detecting passengers who might pose a risk to aviation security. Furthermore, decades of peer-reviewed, published research on the complexities associated with detecting deception through human observation also draw into question the scientific underpinnings of TSA's behavior detection activities. While DHS commissioned a 2011 study to help demonstrate the validity of its approach, the study's findings cannot be used to demonstrate the effectiveness of SPOT because of methodological limitations in the study's design and data collection.

While TSA has several efforts under way to assess the behavioral indicators and expand its collection of data to develop performance metrics for its behavioral detection activities, these efforts are not expected to be completed for several years, and TSA has indicated that additional resources are needed to complete them. Consequently, after 10 years of implementing and testing the SPOT program, TSA cannot demonstrate that the agency's behavior detection activities can reliably and effectively identify high-risk passengers who may pose a threat to the U.S. aviation system.

MATTER FOR CONGRESSIONAL CONSIDERATION

To help ensure that security-related funding is directed to programs that have demonstrated their effectiveness, Congress should consider the findings in this chapter regarding the absence of scientifically validated evidence for using behavioral indicators to identify aviation security threats when assessing the potential benefits of behavior detection activities relative to their cost when making future funding decisions related to aviation security.

RECOMMENDATION FOR EXECUTIVE ACTION

To help ensure that security-related funding is directed to programs that have demonstrated their effectiveness, we recommend that the Secretary of Homeland Security direct the TSA Administrator to limit future funding support for the agency's behavior detection activities until TSA can provide scientifically validated evidence that demonstrates that behavioral indicators can be used to identify passengers who may pose a threat to aviation security.

AGENCY AND THIRD-PARTY COMMENTS AND OUR EVALUATION

We provided a draft of this chapter to DHS and the Department of Justice (DOJ) for review and comment. We also provided excerpts of this chapter to subject matter experts for their review to ensure that the information in the chapter was current, correct, and factual. DOJ did not have any comments, and we incorporated technical comments from subject matter experts as appropriate. DHS provided written comments and technical comments, which we incorporated as appropriate.

DHS did not concur with the recommendation to the Secretary of Homeland Security that directed the TSA Administrator to limit future funding support for the agency's behavior detection activities until TSA can provide scientifically validated evidence that demonstrates that behavioral indicators can be used to identify passengers who may pose a threat to aviation security. Citing concerns with the findings and conclusions, DHS identified two main areas where it disagreed with information presented in the chapter: (1) the findings related to the SPOT validation study and (2) the findings related to the research literature. Further, DHS provided information on its investigation of profiling allegations. We disagree with the statements DHS made in its letter, as discussed in more detail below.

With regard to the findings related to the SPOT validation study, DHS stated in its letter that we used different statistical techniques when we replicated the analysis of SPOT indicators as presented in the DHS April 2011 validation study, a course of action that introduced error into our analysis and resulted in "misleading" conclusions. We disagree with this statement. As described in the chapter, we obtained the validation study dataset from the DHS contractor and replicated the analyses using the same techniques that the contractor used to conduct its analyses of SPOT indicators.[103] As an extra step, in addition to replicating the approach (split-samples) used by the contractors, as described in appendixes II and III of this chapter, we extended those analyses using the full sample of referral data to increase our ability to detect significant associations. In both the replication of the study analyses and the extended analyses we conducted, we found essentially the same result in one aspect as the validation study—that some SPOT behavioral indicators were positively and significantly related to one or more of the outcome measures. Specifically, the validation study reported that 14 of the 41 SPOT behavioral indicators were positively and significantly related, and we found that 18 of the 41 behavioral indicators were positively and significantly related. However, the findings regarding negatively and significantly related SPOT indicators were *not* consistent between the analyses we conducted and the validation study. Specifically, we found that 20 of the 41 behavioral indicators were negatively and significantly related to one or more of the study outcomes (see app. II). That is, we identified 20 SPOT behavioral indicators that were more commonly associated with passengers who were not identified as high-risk passengers than with passengers who were identified as high-risk passengers. In other words, some of the SPOT indicators that behavior detection officers are trained to detect are associated with passengers who were defined by DHS as low risk. Our results were not consistent with the validation study, because the study did not report any indicators that were negatively and significantly correlated with one or more of the outcome measures.[104] Further, because of limitations with the SPOT referral data that we reported in May 2010 and again in this chapter, the data the validation study used to examine behavioral indicators were not sufficiently reliable for use in conducting a statistical analysis of the association between the indicators and high-risk passenger outcomes. We did use these data in order to replicate the validation study findings.

Further, DHS stated in its letter that the TAC agreed with the study's conclusion that SPOT was substantially better at identifying high-risk passengers than a random screening protocol. However, we disagree with this statement. While the TAC report stated that TAC members had few methodological concerns with the way the contractor carried out its research, the members did not receive detailed information on the study, including the validation study data and the final report containing the SPOT validation study results. Specifically, as discussed in our report and cited in the TAC report, multiple TAC members had concerns about some of the conclusions in the validation study and suggested that the contractor responsible for completing the study consider not reporting on some of its results and moving the results to an appendix, rather than including them as a featured portion of the chapter.

Moreover, since the TAC did not receive detailed information about the contents of the SPOT referral report, the individual indicators used in the SPOT program, the validation study data, or the final report containing complete details of the SPOT validation study results, the TAC did not have access to all of the information that we used in our analysis. As discussed in our report, the TAC report noted that several TAC members felt that this lack of information hampered their ability to perform their assigned tasks. Thus, we continue to believe that our conclusion related to the validation study results is valid, and contrary to DHS's statement, we do not believe that the study provides useful data in understanding behavior detection.

With regard to the findings related to the research literature, DHS stated in its letter that we did not consider all the research that was available and that S&T had conducted research—while not published in academic circles for peer review because of various security concerns—that supported the use of behavior detection. DHS also stated that research cited in the chapter "lacked ecological and external validity," because it did not relate to the use of behavior detection in an airport security environment. We disagree. Specifically, as described in the chapter, we reviewed several documents on behavior detection research that S&T and TSA officials provided to us, including an unclassified and a classified literature review that S&T had commissioned. Further, after meetings in June and July 2013, S&T officials provided additional studies, which we reviewed and included in the chapter as applicable. We also included research in the chapter on the use of behavioral indicators that correspond closely to indicators identified in SPOT procedures as indicative of stress, fear, or deception. These studies, many of which were included in the meta-analyses we reviewed, were conducted in a variety of settings— including high-stakes situations where the consequences are great, such as a police interview with an accused murderer—and with different types of individuals—including law enforcement personnel. The meta-analyses we reviewed—which collectively included research from over 400 separate studies related to detecting deception conducted over the past 60 years—found that the ability of human observers to accurately identify deceptive behavior based on behavioral cues or indicators is the same as or slightly better than chance (54 percent).

Further, in its letter, DHS cited a 2013 RAND report, which concluded that there is current value and unrealized potential for using behavioral indicators as part of a system to detect attacks. We acknowledge that behavior detection holds promise for use in certain circumstances and in conjunction with certain other technologies. However, the RAND report DHS cited in its letter refers to behavioral indicators that are defined and used significantly more broadly than those in the SPOT program.[105] The indicators reviewed in the RAND report are neither used in the SPOT program, nor could be used in real time in an airport environment.[106] Further, the RAND report findings cannot be used to support TSA's use of behavior detection activities because the study stated that it could not make a determination of SPOT's effectiveness because information on the program was not in the public domain.

DHS also stated in its letter that it has several efforts under way to improve its behavior detection program and the methodologies used to evaluate it, including the optimization of its behavior detection procedures and plans to begin testing by the third quarter of fiscal year 2014 using robust test and evaluation methods similar to the operational testing conducted in support of technology acquisitions as part of its 3-year performance metrics plan. We are encouraged by TSA's plans in this area. However, TSA did not provide supporting documentation accompanying these plans describing how it will incorporate robust data collection and authentication protocols, as discussed in DHS's letter. Such documentation is to be completed prior to beginning any operational testing. These documents might include a test and evaluation master plan that would describe, among other things, the tests that needed to be conducted to determine system technical performance, operational effectiveness or suitability, and any limitations.[107]

Additionally, in its letter, DHS stated that the omission of research related to verbal indicators of deception was misleading because a large part of BDOs' work is interacting with passengers and assessing whether passengers' statements match their behaviors, or if the passengers' trip stories are in agreement with their travel documents and accessible property. While BDOs' interactions with passengers may elicit useful information, SPOT procedures indicate that casual conversation— voluntary informal interviews conducted by BDOs with passengers referred for additional screening—is conducted *after* the passengers have been selected for a SPOT referral, not as a basis for selecting the passengers for referral. Further, since these interviews are voluntary, passengers are under no obligation to respond to the BDOs questions, and thus information on passengers may not be systematically collected. As noted in our report, promising research on behavioral indicators cited in the RAND report and other literature is focused on using indicators in combination with automated technologies and certain interview techniques, such as asking unanticipated questions. However, when interviewing referred passengers for additional screening, BDOs do not currently have access to the automated technologies discussed in the RAND report.

Further, DHS stated that the goal of the SPOT program is to identify individuals exhibiting behavior indicative of simple emotions such as fear or stress and reroute them to a higher level of screening, and does not attempt to specifically identify persons engaging in lying or terrorist acts. However, DHS also stated in its response that "SPOT uses a broader array of indicators, including stress and fear detection as they relate to high-stakes situations where the consequences are great, for example, suicide attack missions." As noted in the chapter, TSA's program and budget documents associated with behavior detection activities identify that the purpose of these activities is to identify high-risk passengers based on behavioral indicators that indicate mal-intent. For example, the strategic plan notes that in concert with other security measures, behavior detection activities "must be dedicated to finding individuals with the intent to do harm, as well as individuals with connections to terrorist networks that may be involved in criminal activity supporting terrorism." The conclusions, which were confirmed in discussions with subject matter experts and an independent review of studies, indicate that scientifically validated evidence does not support whether the use of behavioral indicators by unaided human observers can be used to identify passengers who may pose a threat to aviation security. DHS also cited the National Research Council's 2008 report to support its use of SPOT.[108] The National Research Council report, which we reviewed as part of our 2010 review of the SPOT program, noted that behavior and appearance monitoring might be able to play a useful role in counterterrorism efforts but also stated that a scientific consensus does not exist regarding whether any behavioral surveillance or physiological monitoring techniques are ready for use in the counterterrorist context, given the present state of the science.[109] According to the National Research Council report, an information-based program, such as a behavior detection program, should first determine if a scientific foundation exists and use scientifically valid criteria to evaluate its effectiveness before going forward. The chapter also stated that programs should have a sound experimental basis, and documentation on the program's effectiveness should be reviewed by an independent entity capable of evaluating the supporting scientific evidence.

With regard to information provided related to profiling, DHS stated that DHS's OIG completed an investigation at the request of TSA into allegations that surfaced at Boston Logan Airport and concluded that these allegations could not be substantiated. However, while the OIG's July 2013 report of investigation on behavior detection officers in Boston concluded that "there was no indication that BDOs racially profiled passengers in order to meet production quotas," the OIG's report also stated that there was evidence of "appearance profiling."[110]

In stating its nonconcurrence with the recommendation to limit future funding in support of its behavior detection activities, DHS stated that TSA's overall security program is composed of interrelated parts, and to disrupt one piece of the multilayered approach may have an adverse impact on other pieces. Further, DHS stated that the behavior detection program should continue to be funded at current levels to allow BDOs to screen passengers while the optimization process proceeds. We disagree. As noted in the chapter, TSA has not developed the performance measures that would allow it to assess the effectiveness of its behavior detection activities compared with other screening methods, such as physical screening. As a result, the impact of behavior detection activities on TSA's overall security program is unknown. Further, not all screening methods are present at every airport, and TSA has modified the screening procedures and equipment used at airports over time. These modifications have included the discontinuance of screening equipment that was determined to be unneeded or ineffective.

Therefore, we continue to believe that providing scientifically validated evidence that demonstrates that behavioral indicators can be used to identify passengers who may pose a threat to aviation security is critical to the implementation of TSA's behavior detection activities. Further, OMB guidance highlights the importance of using resources on programs that have been rigorously evaluated and determined to be effective, and best practices for program management of acquisitions state that technologies should be demonstrated to work reliably in their intended environment prior to program deployment.[111] Consequently, we have added a matter for congressional consideration to this chapter to help ensure that TSA provides information, including scientifically validated evidence, which supports the continued use of its behavior detection activities in identifying threats to aviation security.

Stephen M. Lord
Director, Homeland Security and Justice

Appendix I: Information on Recent Allegations of Passenger Profiling and TSA's Actions to Address Such Allegations

According to the Screening of Passengers by Observation Techniques (SPOT) program's standard operating procedures, behavior detection officers (BDO) must apply the SPOT behavioral indicators to passengers without regard to race, color, religion, national origin, ethnicity, sexual orientation, or disability.[1]

Since 2010, the Transportation Security Administration (TSA) and the Department of Homeland Security's (DHS) Office of Inspector General (OIG) have examined allegations of the use of profiling related to the race, ethnicity, or nationality of passengers by behavior detection officers (BDO) at three airports—Newark Liberty International Airport (Newark), Honolulu International Airport (Honolulu), and Boston Logan International Airport (Boston)—and TSA has taken action to address these allegations. Specifically, in January 2010, TSA concluded an internal investigation at Newark of allegations that BDOs used specific criteria related to the race, ethnicity, or nationality of passengers in order to select and search those passengers more extensively than would have occurred without the use of these criteria. The investigation was conducted by a team of two BDO managers from Boston to determine whether two BDO managers at Newark had established quotas for SPOT referrals to evaluate the performance of their subordinate BDOs.[2] The investigation also sought to determine whether these managers at Newark encouraged profiling of passengers in order to meet quotas that they had established. The investigating team concluded that no evidence existed to support the allegation of a quota system, but noted widespread BDO perception that higher referral rates led to promotion, and that the "overwhelming majority of BDOs" expressed concern that the BDO managers' "focus was solely on increasing the number of referrals and LEO calls." The investigating team said the information collected regarding the allegation of profiling resulted in a reasonable conclusion that that such activity was both directed and affected on a limited basis at Newark, based on one manager's inappropriate direction to BDOs regarding profiling of passengers, racial comments, and the misuse of information intended for situational awareness purposes only.[3] According to TSA officials, disciplinary action taken against this manager resulted in the manager's firing.

Additionally, in 2011, TSA's Office of Inspection (OOI) conducted an investigation of racial profiling allegations against BDOs at Honolulu. The investigation consisted of a review of Equal Employment Opportunity (EEO) complaints, and OOI did not find evidence to support the profiling allegations in the SPOT program.[4]

In July 2012, OOI conducted a compliance inspection at Boston, during which allegations of profiling by BDOs surfaced. Specifically, during interviews with inspectors, allegations surfaced that BDOs were profiling passengers for the purpose of raising the number of law enforcement referrals. These accusations included written complaints from BDOs who claimed other BDOs were selecting passengers for referral screening based on their ethnic or racial appearance, rather than on the basis of the SPOT behavioral indicators and were reported in a September 2012 OOI memorandum. These allegations were referred to the OIG, and in August 2012, the OIG opened an investigation into these profiling allegations in Boston. According to OIG officials, its investigation was completed and its final report was provided to TSA in August 2013.

In August 2012, the Secretary of Homeland Security issued a memorandum directing TSA to take a number of actions in response to allegations of racial profiling by BDOs. These actions include (1) a revision of the SPOT standard operating procedures to, among other things, clarify that passengers who are unwilling or uncomfortable with participating in an interactive discussion and responding to questions will not be pressured by BDOs to do so; (2) refresher training for all BDOs that reinforces antidiscrimination requirements; and (3) TSA communication with BDO supervisors that performance appraisals should not depend on achieving either a high number of referrals or on the arrest rate coming from those referrals, but rather from demonstrated vigilance and skill in applying the SPOT procedures. As of June 2013, TSA, together with the DHS Acting Officer for Civil Rights and Civil Liberties and Counsel to the Secretary of Homeland Security, had completed several of these action items and others were under way. For example, the Secretary of Homeland Security sent a memo to all DHS component heads in April 2013 stating that it is DHS's policy to prohibit the consideration of race or ethnicity in DHS's investigation, screening, and enforcement activities in all but the most exceptional instances.[5]

During our visits to four airports, we asked a random sample of 25 BDOs at the airports to what extent they had seen BDOs in their airport referring passengers based on race, national origin, or appearance rather than behaviors. These responses are not generalizable to the entire BDO population at SPOT airports. Of the 25 randomly selected BDOs we interviewed, 20 said they had not witnessed profiling, and 5 BDOs (including at least 1 from each of the four airports we visited) said that profiling was occurring at their airports, according to their personal observations. Also, 7 additional BDOs contacted us over the course of our review to express concern about the profiling of passengers that they had witnessed. We did not substantiate these specific claims.

In an effort to further assess the race, sex, and national origin of passengers who were referred by BDOs for additional screening, we analyzed the available information in the SPOT referral database and the Federal Air Marshal Service's (FAMS) Transportation Information Sharing System (TISS) database.[6] However, we found that the SPOT referral database does not allow for the recording of information such as race or gender.[7] Without recording these data for every referral, it is difficult to disprove or substantiate such accusations. Since program-wide data on race were not available in the SPOT database, we analyzed a subset of available arrest data that were entered into the TISS database, which allows for race to be recorded.[8] However, because there is not a unique identifier to link referrals from the SPOT database to information entered into TISS, we experienced obstacles when we attempted to match the two databases.[9] For the SPOT referrals we were able to match, we found that data on race were inconsistently recorded in TISS. The limitations associated with matching the two databases and the incompleteness of the race data in TISS made analyzing trends or anomalies in the data impractical.

In March 2013, BDA officials stated that they had initiated a feasibility study to determine the efficacy of collecting data on the race and national origin of passengers referred by BDOs. A pilot is to be conducted at approximately five airports, which have not yet been selected, to collect data and examine whether this type of data collection is feasible and if the data can be used to identify any airport-specific or system-wide trends in referrals. According to BDA officials, the purpose of this study is to examine whether disparities exist in the referral trends, and if so, whether these differences suggest discrimination or bias in the referral process. This pilot is to also include an analysis of the broader demographics of the flying public—not just those referred by BDOs for additional screening—which is information that TSA had not previously collected. Having additional information on the characteristics of the flying public that may be used to compare to the characteristics of those passengers referred by the SPOT program—if TSA determines these data can feasibly be collected—could help enable TSA to reach reasonable conclusions about whether allegations of passenger profiling can be substantiated.

APPENDIX II: OUR ANALYSIS OF VALIDATION STUDY DATA ON SPOT BEHAVIORAL INDICATORS

The validation study reported that 14 of the 41 SPOT behavioral indicators were positively and significantly related to one or more of the study outcomes, but did not report that any of the indicators were negatively and significantly related to the outcome measures.[1] That is, passengers exhibiting the SPOT behaviors that were positively and significantly related were more likely to be arrested, to possess fraudulent documents, or possess prohibited or illegal items. Conversely, passengers exhibiting the behaviors that were negatively and significantly related were less likely to be arrested, to possess fraudulent documents, or possess serious prohibited or illegal items than those who did not exhibit the behavior. While recognizing that the SPOT referral data used in this analysis were potentially unreliable, we replicated the SPOT indicator analysis with the full set of SPOT referral cases from January 1, 2006, to October 31, 2010, and found, consistent with the validation study, that 18 of the 41 behavioral indicators were positively and significantly related to one or more of the outcome measures.[2] We also found, however, that 20 of the 41 behavioral indicators were negatively and significantly related to one or more of the study outcomes.[3] That is, we identified 20 SPOT behavioral indicators that were more commonly associated with passengers who were not identified as high-risk passengers, than with passengers who were identified as high-risk passengers. Of the 41 behavioral indicators in the analysis, almost half of the passengers referred by BDOs for referral screening exhibited one indicator.

APPENDIX III: OBJECTIVES, SCOPE, AND METHODOLOGY

Objectives

This chapter addresses the following questions:

1) To what extent does available evidence support the use of behavioral indicators to identify aviation security threats?
2) To what extent does TSA have data necessary to assess the effectiveness of the SPOT program in identifying threats to aviation security?

In addition, this chapter provides information on TSA's response to recent allegations of racial profiling in the SPOT program, which can be found in appendix I.

Overview of Our Scope and Methodology

To obtain background information and identify changes in the SPOT program since our May 2010 report, we conducted a literature search to identify relevant reports, studies, and articles on passenger screening and deceptive behavior detection.[1] We reviewed program documents in place during the period October 2010 through June 2013, including SPOT standard operating procedures, behavior detection officer performance standards and guidance, a strategic plan, and a performance metrics plan. We met with headquarters TSA and Behavior Detection and Analysis (BDA) program officials to determine the extent to which TSA had implemented recommendations in our May 2010 report and obtain an update on the SPOT program. In addition, we met with officials from U.S. Customs and Border Protection and the Federal Bureau of Investigation (FBI) Behavioral Science Unit to determine the extent to which they use behavior detection techniques. We also interviewed officials in DHS's OIG, who were working on a related audit.[2]

We analyzed data for fiscal years 2011 and 2012 from TSA's SPOT referral database, which is to record all incidents in which BDOs refer passengers for additional screening, including the airport, time and date of the referral, the names of the BDOs involved in the referral, BDOs' observation of the passengers' behaviors, and any actions taken by law enforcement officers, if applicable.[3] We also analyzed data for fiscal years 2011 and 2012 from the FAMS Transportation Information Sharing System (TISS) database, which is a law enforcement database designed to retrieve, assess, and disseminate intelligence information regarding transportation security to FAMS and other federal, state, and local law enforcement agencies.[4] We reviewed available documentation on these databases, such as user guides, data audit reports, and training materials, and interviewed individuals responsible for maintaining these systems. In addition, we analyzed data on BDOs working at airports during this 2-year period, such as date started at TSA, date started as BDO, race, gender, and performance rating scores from TSA's Office of Human Capital, and data on the number of hours worked by these BDOs provided by TSA's Office of Security Operations officials and drawn from the U.S. Department of Agriculture's National Finance Center database, which handles payroll and personnel data for TSA and other federal agencies. Further, we analyzed financial data from fiscal years 2007 through 2012 provided by BDA to determine the expenditures associated with the SPOT program. Additional information about steps we took to assess the reliability of these data is discussed below. We interviewed BDA officials in the Office of Security Capabilities and the Office of Human Capital on the extent to which they collect and analyze these data.

We conducted visits to four airports—Orlando International in Orlando, Florida; Detroit Metropolitan Wayne County in Detroit, Michigan; Logan

International in Boston, Massachusetts; and John F. Kennedy International in New York City, New York. We selected this nonprobability sample based on the airports' size and participation in behavior detection programs.[5] As part of our visits, we interviewed a total of 25 BDOs using a semi-structured questionnaire, and their responses are not generalizable to the entire BDO population at SPOT airports. These BDOs were randomly selected from a list of BDOs on duty at the time of our visit. We interviewed BDO managers and TSA airport managers, such as federal security directors, who oversee the SPOT program at the airports. In addition, to obtain law enforcement officials' perspectives on the SPOT program and their experiences in responding to SPOT referrals, we interviewed officials from the local airport law enforcement agency with jurisdiction at the four airports we visited (Orlando Police Department, Wayne County Airport Authority, Massachusetts State Police, and Port Authority of New York and New Jersey) and federal law enforcement officials assigned to the airports, including U.S. Customs and Border Protection, the FBI, and U.S. Immigration and Customs Enforcement. In nonprobability sampling, a sample is selected from knowledge of the population's characteristics or from a subset of a population where some units in the population have no chance, or an unknown chance, of being selected. A nonprobability sample may be appropriate to provide illustrative examples, or to provide some information on a specific group within a population, but it cannot be used to make inferences about a population or generalize about the population from which the sample is taken. The results of our visits and interviews provided perspectives about the effectiveness of the SPOT program from local airport officials and opportunities to independently observe TSA's behavior detection activities at airports, among other things.

Validation Study

To assess the soundness of the methodology and conclusions in the DHS April 2011 validation study, we reviewed the validation study and Technical Advisory Committee (TAC) final reports and appendixes, and other documents, such as the contractor's proposed study designs, contracts to conduct the study, data collection training materials, and interim reports on data monitoring visits and study results. We assessed these efforts with established practices in designing evaluations and generally accepted statistical principles.[6] We obtained the validation study datasets from the contractor and replicated several of the analyses, based on the methodology described in the final report. Generally, we replicated the study's split-sample analyses, and as an extra step, extended those analyses using the full sample of SPOT referral data, as discussed below and in appendix II. In addition, we interviewed headquarters TSA, BDA, and Science and Technology Directorate (S&T) officials responsible for the validation study, representatives from the contractor who conducted the study, and 8 of the 12 members of the TAC who commented on and evaluated the adequacy of the validation study and issued a separate report in June 2011.[7]

Data Reliability

To assess the reliability of the SPOT referral data, we reviewed relevant documentation, including privacy impact assessments and a 2012 data audit of the SPOT database, and interviewed TSA and BDA headquarters and field officials about the controls in place to maintain the integrity of the data. To determine the extent to which the SPOT database is accurate and complete, we reviewed the data in accordance with established procedures for assessing data reliability and conducted tests, such as electronic tests to determine if there were anomalies in the dataset (such as out-of-range dates and missing data) and reviewed a sample of certain coded data fields and compared them with narrative information in the open text fields.[8] We determined that the data for fiscal years 2011 and 2012 across the 49 airports in our scope were sufficiently reliable for us to use to reflect the total number of SPOT referrals and arrests made, and to standardize the referral and arrest data, based on the number of hours each BDO spent performing operational SPOT activities.[9]

In October 2012, TSA completed an audit of the data contained in the SPOT referral database in which it identified common errors, such as missing data fields and incorrect point totals. According to the 2012 audit, for the time period of March 1, 2010, through August 31, 2012, covering more than 108,000 referrals, the SPOT referral database had an overall error rate of 7.96 percent, which represented more than 8,600 known errors and more than 14,000 potential errors. According to TSA, the agency has begun taking steps to reduce this error rate, including visits to airports with significant data integrity issues and the development of a new SPOT referral database that is designed to prevent the most common errors from occurring. BDA officials told us that they have begun steps toward a nationwide rollout of their new system in May 2013, which includes pilots and developing procedures to mandate airports' use of the system. On the basis of our review of the types of errors identified by the data audit, we determined that the SPOT referral data were sufficiently reliable for us to analyze BDO referral rates. However, the audit identifies problems with arrest data, which is one of the three categories of "potential errors." The audit does not report on the magnitude of this error category, because identifying these errors requires a manual audit of the data at the airport level. As a result, we determined that the arrest data were not reliable enough for us to report on details about the arrests.

Use of Behavioral Indicators

To determine the extent to which available evidence exists to support the use of behavioral indicators to identify security threats, we analyzed research on behavioral indicators, reviewed the validation study findings on behavioral indicators, and analyzed SPOT referral data.

Research on Behavioral Indicators

Working from a literature review of articles from 2003 to 2013 that were identified using search terms such as "behavior detection deception," and discussions with researchers who had published articles in this area, we contacted other researchers to interview and academic and government research to review.[10] While the results of our interviews cannot be used to generalize about all research on behavior deception detection, they represent a mix of researchers and views by virtue of their affiliation with various academic institutions and governments, authorship of meta-analyses on these issues, and subject matter expertise in particular research areas.

We also reviewed more than 40 articles and books on behavior-based deception detection dating from 1999 to 2013. These articles, books, and reports were identified by our literature search of databases, such as ArticleFirst, ECO, WorldCat, ProQuest, and Academic One File and recommendations by TSA and the experts we interviewed. Through our discussions and research, we identified four meta-analyses, which used an approach for statistically cumulating the results of several studies to answer questions about program impacts. These meta-analyses analyzed "effect sizes" across several studies—the measure of the difference in outcome between a treatment group and a comparison group.[11] For example, these meta-analyses measured the accuracy of an individual's deception judgments when assessing another individual's credibility in terms of the percentage that lies and truths were correctly classified and the impact of various factors on the accuracy of deception judgments, such as the liar's motivation or expertise of the individual making the judgment. We reviewed the methodologies of 4 meta-analyses covering over 400 separate studies on detection deception over a 60-year period, including whether an appropriate evaluation approach was selected for each meta-analysis, and whether the data were collected and analyzed in ways that allowed valid conclusions to be drawn, in accordance with established practices in evaluation design.[12] In addition, we interviewed two authors of these meta-analyses to ensure that the analyses were sound and we determined that the analyses were sufficiently reliable for describing what evidence existed to support the use of behavioral indicators to identify security threats. We determined that the research we identified was sufficiently reliable for describing the evidence that existed regarding the use of behavioral indicators to identify security threats.

Further, we reviewed documents developed by TSA and other foreign countries as part of an international study group to assess TSA's efforts to identify best practices on the use of behavioral detection in an airport environment.

Validation Study Results on SPOT Indicators

To assess the soundness of the methodology and conclusions in the April 2011 validation study finding that 14 of the 41 SPOT indicators were related to outcomes that indicate a possible threat, we reviewed evidence supporting our May 2010 conclusions that the SPOT referral database lacked controls to help ensure the completeness and accuracy of the data. We interviewed TSA officials and obtained documentation, such as a data audit report and a functional requirements document, to determine the extent to which problems in the SPOT database were being addressed. We also reviewed the June 2011 TAC final report and interviewed contractor officials regarding analysis limitations because of data sparseness, or low frequency of occurrences of indicators in the SPOT database.

We also obtained the dataset used in the study—SPOT referral data from January 2006 through October 2010—and replicated the SPOT indicator analyses described in the study. Although we found that the data were not sufficiently reliable for use in conducting a statistical analysis of the association between the indicators and high-risk passenger outcomes, we used the data to assess the study's methodology and conclusions. The dataset included a total of 247,630 SPOT referrals from 175 airports. As described in the validation study, we calculated whether the odds on each of the four study outcome measures—LEO arrest, possession of fraudulent documents, possession of a serious prohibited or illegal item, or the combination of all three measures—were associated with the 41 SPOT indicators. These odd ratios were derived from four sets of 41 separate cross-tabulations—2 x 2 tables—in which each of the four outcomes is cross-classified by each of the

41 individual indicators. Odds ratios greater than 1.0 indicate positive associations, that is, passengers exhibiting the behavior were more likely to be arrested, to possess fraudulent documents, or to possess serious prohibited or illegal items. On the other hand, odds ratios of less than 1.0 indicate negative associations, that is, passengers exhibiting the behavior were less likely to be arrested, to possess fraudulent documents, or to possess serious prohibited or illegal items than those who do not exhibit the behavior. The number of positive and significant associations we detected was slightly larger than the number reported in the validation study mainly because we reported results from an analysis of the full sample of SPOT referrals—a total of 247,630 SPOT passenger referrals. In contrast, the validation study stated that a split-sample approach was used, in which each years' dataset was split into two stratified random subsets across the years and analyses were conducted independently on each aggregated subset. The validation study stated that this approach allowed an examination of the extent to which results may vary across each subset and to address possible random associations in the data. The validation study further stated that this was important because changes in the SPOT program, such as fewer airports and BDOs involved in the earlier years and small changes to the SPOT instrument in March 2009, could have affected the analyses. However, after replicating the split-sample approach, we determined that it was not the most appropriate one to use because it substantially diminished the power to detect significant associations in light of how infrequently referrals occurred. We report the results of our analyses of the full sample of SPOT referrals that indicate behavioral indicators that are positively and significantly related, as well as negatively and significantly related, in the behavioral indicator section of the chapter and in appendix II.

SPOT Referral Data

To determine the extent to which SPOT referrals varied by BDOs across airports for fiscal years 2011 and 2012, we initially selected the 50 airports identified by TSA's May 2012 Current Airports Threat Assessment report as having the highest probability of threat from terrorist attacks. We chose to limit the scope of our review to the top 50 airports because the majority of the BDOs are deployed to these airports; and they account for 68 percent of the passenger throughput, and 75 percent of SPOT referrals. To standardize the referral rates across airports, we calculated the number of SPOT referrals by individual BDOs and matched these BDOs by the number of hours that particular BDOs spent performing SPOT activities.[13] San Francisco International Airport was in the initial selection of 50 airports; however, we excluded San Francisco International because the hourly data provided to us for San Francisco BDOs, who are managed by a screening contractor, were not comparable with the hourly data provided to us for TSA-managed BDOs.[14] The scope of our analysis was then 49 SPOT airports.

To calculate BDO hours spent performing SPOT activities, we analyzed BDO time and attendance data provided by TSA for fiscal years 2011 and 2012 from the U.S. Department of Agriculture's National Finance Center. We limited our analysis to the hours BDOs spent performing SPOT activities because it is primarily during these times that BDOs make SPOT referrals. Thus, BDO hours charged to activities such as leave, baggage screening, or cargo inspection activities were excluded. For example, we found that BDOs had charged time to cargo inspection activities that were unrelated to the SPOT program. These inspections are carried out under TSA's Compliance Division in the Office of Security Operations, and are designed to ensure compliance with transportation security regulations. We also limited our analysis to nonmanager BDOs, as managers are not regularly engaged in making referrals. Finally, about 55 BDOs, or about 2 percent of the approximately 2,400 BDOs (including both managers and nonmanagers), were not included in our analysis because we could not reconcile their names with time and attendance data after several attempts with TSA officials. We calculated average referral rates per 160 hours worked, or about 4 40-hour weeks, across 2,199 BDOs working at 49 airports, and a referral rate for each airport.

To better understand the variation in referral rates, we conducted a multivariate analysis to determine whether certain variables affected SPOT referral rates and LEO referral rates, including airports at which BDOs worked during fiscal years 2011 and 2012; BDO annual performance scores for 2011 and 2012; years of experience with TSA and as a BDO; and demographic information on BDOs, such as age, gender, race, and highest educational level attained at the time of employment. Although multivariate methods do not allow us to establish that referral rates are causally related to the BDO characteristics we had information about, they allowed us to examine the associations between referral rates and the different specific BDOs while controlling for other BDO characteristics, including the airports in which the BDOs worked.

Moreover, the methods we employed allowed us to determine whether the observed differences in the sample data were different more than by merely chance fluctuations. Our statistical models and estimates are sensitive to our choice of variables; thus, researchers testing different variables may find different results. See appendix IV for additional information on the results of our analyses.

Data to Assess Effectiveness of SPOT

To determine the extent to which TSA has data necessary to assess the effectiveness of the SPOT program in identifying threats to aviation security, we reviewed the validation study's findings comparing passengers selected by SPOT with randomly selected passengers, analyzed TSA plans and analyses designed to measure SPOT's effectiveness, and analyzed data on SPOT referrals and LEO arrests.

Validation Study Results Comparing Passengers Selected by SPOT with Randomly Selected Passengers

To assess the soundness of the methodology and conclusions in the April 2011 validation study findings that SPOT was more likely to identify high-risk passengers than a random selection of passengers, we assessed the study design and implementation against established practices for designing evaluations and generally accepted statistical principles. These practices include, for example, probability sample methods, data collection and monitoring procedures, and quasi-experimental design.[15] We obtained the validation study datasets and replicated the study findings, based on the methodology described in the final report. Further, we analyzed the validation study data from December 1, 2009, to October 31, 2010, on passengers who were referred to a LEO and who were ultimately arrested. To the extent possible, we reviewed SPOT data to determine the reasons for the arrest and if there were differences between arrested passengers who were referred by SPOT and arrested passengers who were randomly selected.

TSA Performance Data

To determine the extent to which TSA has plans to collect and analyze performance data to assess SPOT's overall effectiveness, we reviewed TSA's efforts to inform the future direction of BDA and the SPOT program, such as a return-on-investment and risk-based allocation analyses. We evaluated TSA's efforts against DHS, GAO, and other guidance regarding these analyses.[16] For example, we reviewed TSA's return-on-investment analysis against the analytical standards in the Office of Management and Budget's Circular A-94, which provides guidance on conducting benefit-cost and cost-effectiveness analyses.[17] We also reviewed documentation associated with program oversight, including a 2012 performance metrics plan, and evaluated TSA's efforts to collect and analyze data to provide oversight of BDA and the SPOT program against criteria in Office of Management and Budget guidance and *Standards for Internal Control in the Federal Government.*[18] Further, we reviewed performance work statements in TSA contracts to determine the extent to which the contractor's work is to fulfill the tasks in TSA's performance metrics plan. Also, we reviewed FAMS law enforcement reports, TISS incident reports, and the SPOT referral database to determine the extent to which information from BDO referrals was used for further investigation to identify potential ties to terrorist investigations. We also analyzed SPOT referral data that TSA uses to track SPOT program activities, including the number of passengers who were referred to a LEO and ultimately arrested for fiscal years 2011 and 2012.

Profiling Allegations

To provide information about how TSA and DHS's OIG have examined allegations of racial and other types of profiling of passengers by BDOs, we reviewed documentation from 2010 to 2013, such as investigation reports, privacy impact assessments, BDO training materials, and TSA memos.[19] To explore the extent to which we could determine the race, gender, and national origin of passengers who were referred by BDOs for additional screening, we analyzed information in the SPOT referral database and the TISS database for fiscal years 2011 and 2012. We reviewed a September 2012 TSA contract that will, among other things, study whether any evidence exists for racial or ethnic profiling in the SPOT program. We also reviewed interim reports produced by the contractor as of June 2013. Because racial profiling allegations in Boston were made during the course of our review, we asked the random sample of 25 BDOs at the four airports we visited to what extent they had seen BDOs in their airport referring passengers based on race, national origin, or appearance rather than behaviors. These responses are not generalizable to the entire BDO population at SPOT airports. Further, 7 additional BDOs contacted us over the course of our review to express concern about the profiling of passengers that they had witnessed. We did not substantiate these specific claims. We also interviewed TSA headquarters and field officials, such as federal security directors and BDO managers, as well as DHS OIG officials.

We conducted this performance audit from April 2012 to November 2013 in accordance with generally accepted government auditing standards. Those standards require that we plan and perform the audit to obtain sufficient, appropriate evidence to provide a reasonable basis for our findings and conclusions based on our audit objectives. We believe the evidence obtained provides a reasonable basis for our findings and conclusions based on our audit objectives.

APPENDIX IV: CHARACTERISTICS AND REFERRAL RATES OF BEHAVIOR DETECTION OFFICERS AT 49 SPOT AIRPORTS

To better understand the variation in referral rates, we analyzed whether certain variables affected SPOT referral rates and LEO referral rates, including BDO characteristics, such as average performance scores for fiscal years 2011 and 2012, years of TSA and BDO experience, age, gender, educational level, years employed at TSA and as a BDO, and race, as well as the airport in which the BDOs worked. As described earlier, these analyses standardized SPOT referral data for 2,199 BDOs across 49 airports for fiscal years 2011 and 2012.

BDO Characteristics and Referral Rates

The characteristics of the 2,199 BDOs in our analyses varied across different categories, as shown in table 3. About 51 percent of the BDOs were under 40 years of age, and slightly more than 25 percent were 50 years or older. Nearly 64 percent of the BDOs joined TSA before the end of 2005, but the majority, or more than 85 percent, became BDOs after the beginning of 2008. Nearly 65 percent of the BDOs were male. Fifty percent were white, about 26 percent were African-American, and about 18 percent were Hispanic. About 65 percent of the BDOs had a high school education or less.[1] The BDOs were distributed unevenly across airports, with the largest numbers in Logan International (Boston), Dallas-Fort Worth International, John F. Kennedy International (New York), Los Angeles International, and O'Hare International (Chicago). Each BDO worked primarily in one airport during the 2-year period. For example, 80 of the 2,199 BDOs, or about 4 percent, worked in multiple airports and the remaining 2,119 BDOs, or 96 percent, worked at one airport during the 2 year time period.

Table 3. Average Screening of Passengers by Observation Techniques (SPOT) Referral Rates and Law Enforcement Official (LEO) Referral Rates at 49 Airports, by Behavior Detection Officer (BDO) Characteristics and Airport, Fiscal Years 2011 and 2012

BDO characteristic	Category	Number of BDOs	Percentage of total BDOs
Average Performance Accountability and Standards System (PASS) scores for 2011 and 2012[a]	Quintile 1 (33.40–82.95)	409	18.6
	Quintile 2 (83.05–88.95)	409	18.6
	Quintile 3 (89.00–93.40)	405	18.4
	Quintile 4 (93.50–97.45)	395	18.0
	Quintile 5 (97.50–105.00)	428	19.5
	Missing data	153	7.0
Age	Under 30 years old	377	17.1
	30 to 39 years old	737	33.5
	40 to 49 years old	499	22.7
	50 years and older	586	26.6
Year began employment as BDO	2005 to 2007	323	14.7
	2008 to 2009	1,330	60.5
	2010 to 2012	546	24.8
Year began employment with TSA	2002 to 2003	886	40.3
	2004 to 2005	518	23.6
	2006 to 2007	539	24.5
	2008 to 2012	256	11.6
Gender	Female	763	34.7
	Male	1,436	65.3
Race	African-American	561	25.5
	Asian	117	5.3
	Hawaiian-Pacific Islander	7	0.3

BDO characteristic	Category	Number of BDOs	Percentage of total BDOs
	Hispanic	386	17.6
	Indian Alaskan Native	21	1.0
	White	1,101	50.1
	Two or more races	5	0.2
	Did not report race	1	0.0
Level of education at time of hire by TSA	High school or less	1,436	65.3
	Some college	512	23.3
	College graduate	251	11.4
Airport where BDO worked	Airport 1	19	0.9
	Airport 2	20	0.9
	Airport 3	72	3.3
	Airport 4	11	0.5
	Airport 5	9	0.4
	Airport 6	89	4.0
	Airport 7	15	0.7
	Airport 8	50	2.3
	Airport 9	27	1.2
	Airport 10	46	2.1
	Airport 11	19	0.9
	Airport 12	30	1.4
	Airport 13	44	2.0
	Airport 14	64	2.9
	Airport 15	86	3.9
	Airport 16	49	2.2
	Airport 17	72	3.3
	Airport 18	55	2.5
	Airport 19	8	0.4
	Airport 20	12	0.5
	Airport 21	33	1.5
	Airport 22	53	2.4
	Airport 23	70	3.2
	Airport 24	30	1.4
	Airport 25	18	0.8
	Airport 26	99	4.5
	Airport 27	70	3.2
	Airport 28	104	4.7
	Airport 29	65	3.0
	Airport 30	63	2.9

Table 3. (Continued)

BDO characteristic	Category	Number of BDOs	Percentage of total BDOs
	Airport 31	31	1.4
	Airport 32	21	1.0
	Airport 33	19	0.9
	Airport 34	59	2.7
	Airport 35	16	0.7
	Airport 36	63	2.9
	Airport 37	99	4.5
	Airport 38	33	1.5
	Airport 39	69	3.1
	Airport 40	58	2.6
	Airport 41	23	1.0
	Airport 42	25	1.1
	Airport 43	36	1.6
	Airport 44	10	0.5
	Airport 45	51	2.3
	Airport 46	21	1.0
	Airport 47	27	1.2
	Airport 48	35	1.6
	Airport 49	21	1.0
	Multiple airports [b]	80	3.6
Total		2,199	100

Source: GAO analysis of TSA data.

[a]BDOs and other transportation security officers' performance is rated annually using a point scoring system under PASS, TSA's pay-for-performance system.

[b]The numbers are BDOs who worked at more than 1 airport during fiscal years 2011 and 2012.

Overall, BDOs averaged about 1.57 SPOT referrals and 0.22 LEO referrals per 160 hours worked. These rates vary across the different BDO categories. However, these differences should be considered cautiously, as differences that appear to exist across categories for one characteristic may be confounded with differences across others. For example, the apparent difference in referral rates between younger and older BDOs may be the result of younger BDOs working disproportionately in airports with higher referral rates.

Multivariate Analysis of SPOT and LEO Referral Rates

To better understand the effects of BDO characteristics, including the airports they worked in, on SPOT referral and LEO referral rates, we conducted simple regression analyses.[2] Overall, the greatest amount of the variation in BDO SPOT referral rates was explained by the airport at which the referral occurred. That is, the BDO's referral rate was associated substantially with the airport at which he or she was conducting SPOT activities.

A number of BDO characteristics were significantly related to the rate of SPOT referrals, both before and after adjustment, or in both bivariate and multivariate models. For example, in multivariate model 2—the model fully adjusted for both BDO characteristics and airport—BDOs with higher PASS scores had significantly higher rates of SPOT referrals than those with lower PASS scores. Other differences, such as BDOs' level of education at the time of hire, were not significantly related to the rate of referrals, after controlling for other factors. BDO characteristics–apart from the airport in which they worked–did not account for much of the variation in SPOT referral rates across BDOs. The R^2 values, or coefficients of determination, indicate that none of the BDO characteristics individually account for more than about 1 percent of that variation, and all of these characteristics collectively account for 3 percent of the variation in SPOT referral rates across BDOs. In contrast, differences in airports were highly significant, even after adjusting for differences in BDO characteristics. For example, BDOs in 2 airports had significantly higher average SPOT referral rates than BDOs in the referent category, by 3.31 and 1.17 referrals per 160 hours worked, respectively. Overall, while other BDO characteristics collectively account for a small percentage of the variation in average SPOT referral rates, the airport in which the BDO worked accounted for a much larger percentage of the variation.

The results for LEO referrals were roughly similar to those for SPOT referrals, with a few minor differences. For example, in contrast to the average rate for SPOT referral analyses, the average rate of LEO referrals was unrelated to the length of service as a BDO. However, as with the SPOT referral analyses, airports were highly significant, with BDOs in a few airports averaging significantly higher rates of referrals than BDOs in the referent category, and BDOs in most of the other airports averaging significantly lower LEO referral rates. Because they were less common, LEO referrals may have been more difficult to predict that SPOT referrals. Differences in the other BDO characteristics— multivariate model 1—collectively accounted for a small percentage of the variation in average LEO referral rates, while differences across airports accounted for a larger percentage.

Airport Throughput Analysis

Separate analyses we conducted revealed that the sizeable and highly significant differences in SPOT referral rates and LEO referral rates across airports were not fully accounted for by differences in the number of passengers who pass through airport checkpoints.

APPENDIX V: TSA'S PERFORMANCE METRICS FOR BEHAVIOR DETECTION AND ANALYSIS

Table 4 shows TSA's proposed performance metrics as detailed in appendix G in its Behavior Detection and Analysis performance metrics plan dated November 2012.

Table 4. Transportation Security Administration's (TSA) Proposed Performance Metrics, November 2012

Category/subcategory	Metric	Description
Human capital management		
Operational management	Percent checkpoint coverage	The percentage of time a behavior detection officer (BDO) is present at a checkpoint while the checkpoint is open, averaged across all checkpoints within an airport
	Number of BDO checkpoint screening hours	The number of hours a full-time equivalent (FTE) spends performing checkpoint screening, broken down by employee type (i.e., BDO and BDO supervisor).
	Number of BDO playbook screening hours	The number of hours an FTE spends performing playbook plays, broken down by employee type (i.e., BDO and BDO supervisor).

Category/subcategory	Metric	Description
		A playbook is a risk mitigation program that makes use of TSA and non-TSA security assets that are deployed in a random or unpredictable manner to complicate terrorist planning activities and deter attacks.
	Number of BDO training hours	The number of hours an FTE spends on training activities, broken down by employee type (i.e., BDO and BDO supervisor).
	Number of BDO mentoring hours	The number of hours an FTE spends on mentoring other BDOs, broken down by employee type (i.e., BDO and BDO supervisor).
	Number of BDO administrator work hours	The number of hours an FTE spends performing administrative work, broken down by employee type (i.e., BDO and BDO supervisor).
	Number of FTE	The total number of FTEs working during a given time interval, broken down by employee type (i.e., BDO and BDO supervisor).
	Number of hours per FTE	The total number of hours worked by an FTE, broken down by employee type (i.e., BDO and BDO supervisor).
	Staff deployment efficiency	The number of days between when a new FTE is hired and when the FTE starts screening travelers in an actual operation setting.
Human factors	Fatigue level	The level of fatigue experienced by BDOs. Factors to be measured are to be finalized by DHS S&T. Initial factors to be considered include average number of hours spent in checkpoint screening tasks prior to a break and the number of passengers processed per FTE.
	Managerial level	The level of managerial presence experienced by BDOs. Factors to be measured are to be finalized during the experimental design process by DHS Science and Technology Directorate (S&T).

Table 4. (Continued)

Category/subcategory	Metric	Description
		Initial factors to be considered include average number of hours spent in the checkpoint area per managerial FTE and the ratio of managerial FTEs to regular FTEs.
	Stimulus level	The level of stimulus presence experienced by BDOs. Factors to be measured are to be finalized during the experimental design process by DHS S&T. Initial factors to be considered include the average number of canines that sniff for explosives in the checkpoint area and the number of warning signs in the checkpoint area.
	Fatigue impact score	The impact varying levels of fatigue have on a BDO's ability to identify SPOT behavior indicators. Fatigue is to be measured using the procedures described for the "fatigue level" metric. The impact on performance is to be measured as a part of an S&T study.
	Managerial presence impact score	The impact varying levels of managerial presence have on a BDO's ability to identify SPOT behavior indicators. Managerial presence is to be measured using the procedures described for the "managerial level" metric. The impact on performance is to be measured as a part of the S&T Indicator Reliability Study.
	Stimulus presence impact score	The impact varying levels of stimulus presence have on a BDO's ability to identify SPOT behavior indicators. Stimulus presence is to be measured using the procedures described for the "stimulus level" metric. The impact on performance is to be measured as a part of the S&T Indicator Reliability Study.

Category/subcategory	Metric	Description
General Performance		
Individual performance	Conversation tools	The BDO's ability to communicate effectively with passengers and team members. Possible factors include: the ability to hold a casual conversation, the ability to ask appropriate questions, team communication, tone, cultural sensitivity, the ability to answer passenger's questions appropriately, and improvisational skills. This metric is to be an aggregated score based on the BDO's performance across the subfactors, once the subfactors have been selected and evaluation criteria for each have been established.
	Cognitive agility	The BDO's ability to sustain a high cognitive load without decreased performance. Possible factors include: ability to reset, ability to observe and interact, attention to details, and alertness. This metric is to be an aggregated score based on the BDO's performance across the subfactors, once the subfactors have been selected and evaluation criteria for each have been established.
	Mission alignment	The BDO's awareness of alignment with TSA's mission. Possible factors include: referral integrity, neutrality, and briefing attendance. This metric is to be an aggregated score based on the BDO's performance across the subfactors, once the subfactors have been selected and evaluation criteria for each have been established.
	Percentage of improvement across individual performance evaluations	The percentage change in a BDO's performance across the various individual performance assessments (Performance Accountability and Standards System, Job Knowledge Test, Proficiency Evaluation Checklist, conversation skills,

Table 4. (Continued)

Category/subcategory	Metric	Description
		cognitive agility, and mission alignment) on a biannual basis.
Security effectiveness		
Probability of detection (P(d))	Significance of relationship between behavioral indicators and high-risk outcomes	The frequency with which a behavior indicator was associated with a known incident of high-risk outcomes (i.e., LEO arrests, LEO referrals, serious prohibited or illegal items, or artful concealment).
	Number of simulated high-risk outcomes detected by SPOT referral screening divided by number of simulated high-risk injected into SPOT referral screening (by high-risk outcome type)	The ratio of high-stakes actors detected by SPOT referral screening to the total number of high-stakes actors introduced by SPOT referral screening, categorized by high-risk outcome type. A high-stakes actor is an actor tasked with performing a specific task intended to simulate the kind of high-stress psychological conditions an adversary would face when trying to pass through security. A detection is any outcome that results in the actor being referred to a LEO, the serious prohibited or illegal item being detected, or the artful concealment being detected.
	Number of high-risk outcomes per BDO referral divided by number of high-risk outcomes per randomized play (by high-risk outcome type)	The number of high-risk outcomes per referral (from SPOT checkpoint screening and playbook plays) divided by the number of high-risk outcomes per randomly selected passenger (randomly selected passengers to perform a play that includes some combination of pat-down and open bag search). This ratio measures how reliable BDOs are at identifying high-risk outcomes in comparison with random selection.

Category/subcategory	Metric	Description
	Variance and standard deviation of SPOT score assigned to the same passenger by different BDOs	The variance and standard deviation of the SPOT score assigned to the same footage of an individual passenger by a set of different BDOs.
	Variance and standard deviation of the number of passengers (from within the same evaluation set) referred by BDOs.	The variance and standard deviation of the number of passengers recommended for referral screening suggested by a set of different BDOs watching the same footage of a checkpoint area. The footage should be selected to include passengers displaying a range of behaviors and should include passengers displaying indicators that meet the referral threshold.
	Number of behavioral indicators identified divided by number of behavioral indicators present	The number of behavioral indicators identified by a BDO divided by the number of behavior indicators the passenger being observed actually displayed. This is a measure of the BDOs ability to recognize the presence of SPOT indicators. The exact mechanism for collecting these data may vary depending on pilot/research results.
	Number of passengers identified for referral divided by number of passengers meeting behavior indicator threshold	The number of passengers identified for referral divided by the number of passengers meeting the behavior indicator threshold. This is a measure of the BDOs' ability to correctly refer passengers who demonstrate behavior indicators beyond the SPOT threshold score. The exact mechanism for collecting these data may vary depending on pilot/research results.
	Significance of relationship between high-risk outcomes and actual terrorists or "mal-intent"	The basis for selecting certain high-risk outcomes as proxies of actual terrorists. This measure is qualitative in nature and is not expected to be precisely measured.

Table 4. (Continued)

Category/subcategory	Metric	Description
	Number of high-risk outcomes caught by BDOs divided by number of high-risk outcomes missed by BDOs	The number of high-risk outcomes detected as a result of BDO intervention divided by the number of high-risk outcomes that went undetected by BDOs.
Probability of encounter (P(e))	Number of passengers screened per hour (in lab setting)	The number of passengers a BDO is able to screen per hour. Screen refers to completing a visual inspection of the passenger, sufficient such that if the passenger were displaying behavior indicators, the BDO is able to detect said indicators. The lab setting of this measure refers to the fact that this metric will be captured using simulated airport traffic conditions for more controlled measurements.
	Number of passengers screened per hour (in operational setting)	The number of passengers a BDO is able to screen per hour. Screen refers to completing a visual inspection of the passenger, sufficient such that if the passenger were displaying behavior indicators, the BDO is able to detect said indicators. The operational setting of this measure refers to the fact that this metric is to be captured during actual airport operations to ensure more realistic test conditions.
	Number of passengers screened by BDOs divided by total throughput	The total number of passengers screened by BDOs divided by the total through put. There are a number of possible ways to approach this question and various scopes to which it can be captured. These characteristics are to be defined through pilot and research results.

Source: TSA, Behavior Detection and Analysis Division (BDAD) Performance Metrics Plan, November 2012.

Table 5. Transportation Security Administration's (TSA) Analysis of Gaps in Existing Behavior Detection and Analysis Performance Metrics Data, November 2012

Category/ subcategory	TSA overall score[a]	Variable	Validity	Reliability	Frequency	Current capability scope	Proposed scope
Human capital management							
Operational management		Percent checkpoint coverage	0	0	0	n/a	Airport
		Number of behavior detection officer (BDO) checkpoint screening hours	1	1	1	Airport	Individual
		Number of BDO playbook screening hours	1	1	1	Airport	Individual
		Number of BDO training hours	3	3	2	Individual	Individual
		Number of BDO mentoring hours	1	3	1	Individual	Individual
		Number of BDO administrator work hours	1	1	1	Airport	Individual
		Number of full-time equivalents (FTE)	1	3	2	Airport	Airport
		Number of hours per FTE	1	3	2	Airport	Airport
		Staff deployment efficiency	0	0	0	n/a	Airport
Human factors		Fatigue level	0	0	0	n/a	National
		Managerial level	0	0	0	n/a	National
		Stimulus level	0	0	0	n/a	National
		Fatigue impact score	0	0	0	n/a	Foundational[b]
		Managerial presence impact score	0	0	0	n/a	Foundational[b]
		Stimulus presence impact score	0	0	0	n/a	Foundational[b]

Table 5. (Continued)

General performance							
Individual performance		Performance Accountability and Standards System (PASS) metrics	2	2	2	Individual	Individual
		Performance Compliance Assessment (PCA) metrics	3	3	1	Individual	Individual
		Job Knowledge Test (JKT) metrics	2	2	2	Individual	Individual
		Proficiency Evaluation Checklist (PEC) metrics	2	2	2	Individual	Individual
		Conversation skills	0	0	0	n/a	Individual
		Cognitive agility	0	0	0	n/a	Individual
		Mission alignment	0	0	0	n/a	Individual
		Percentage of improvement across individual performance evaluations	0	0	0	n/a	Individual
Security effectiveness							
Probability of detection (P(d))		Significance of relationship between behavioral indicators and high-risk outcomes	3	3	1	Foundational[b]	Foundational[b]

Category/ subcategory	TSA overall score[a]	Variable	Validity	Reliability	Frequency	Current capability scope	Proposed scope
		Number of simulated high-risk outcomes detected by Screening of Passengers by Observation Techniques (SPOT) referral screening/number of simulated high-risk injected into SPOT referral screening (by high-risk outcome type)	0	0	0	n/a	National
		Number of high-risk outcomes per BDO referral/number of high-risk outcomes per randomized play (by high-risk outcome type)	0	0	0	n/a	National
		Variance and standard deviation of SPOT score assigned to the same passenger by different BDOs	0	0	0	n/a	National
		Variance and standard deviation of the number of passengers (from within the same evaluation set) referred by BDOs	0	0	0	n/a	National
		Number of behavioral indicators identified/number of behavioral indicators present	0	0	0	n/a	National
		Number of passengers identified for referral/number of passengers meeting behavior indicator threshold	0	0	0	n/a	National
		Significance of relationship between high-risk outcomes and actual terrorists/mal-intent	0	0	0	n/a	Foundational[b]

Table 5. (Continued)

		Number of high-risk outcomes caught by BDOs/number of high-risk outcomes missed by BDOs	0	0	0	n/a	National
		Number of LEO arrests	1	3	2	Airport	Airport
		Number of serious prohibited or illegal items	1	3	2	Airport	Airport
		Number of artfully concealed prohibited items	3	3	2	Airport	Airport
		Number of passengers identified as illegal aliens	1	3	2	Airport	Airport
		Number of referrals	3	3	2	Airport	Airport
Probability of encounter (P(e))		Number of passengers screened per hour (in lab setting)	0	0	0	n/a	Foundational[b]
		Number of passengers screened per hour (in operational setting)	1	1	1	Airport	National
		Number of passengers screened by BDOs/total throughput	0	0	0	n/a	National

Legend:

= TSA overall assessment: Collecting a low level of data needed for performance management. Data are being collected but the data do not directly measure BDO performance or are a weak indicator of BDO performance. There is below 90 percent confidence in the way the metric is collected or the data that are collected do not reliably measure the metric, or the data that are collected can be easily manipulated or inflated to get more desirable results. The ability to collect or calculate the metric is difficult and may have been collected one or two times with no future scheduled recurrence.

= TSA overall assessment: Not collecting or analyzing data needed for performance management. None of the data are being collected for this metric or measure. Data are extremely difficult to collect or TSA does not have the capability to collect the data with any level of confidence.

n/a = Not applicable.

Source: TSA, Behavior Detection and Analysis Division (BDAD) Performance Metrics Plan, November 2012.

[a]TSA's overall score for each subcategory is its overall assessment of the validity, reliability, and frequency scores for each variable within the subcategory.

[b]Foundational measures are to measure the validity of certain concepts related to the program. The findings of foundational measures are not expected to change significantly with time; rather they are to tell the base nature of the variable in question.

Table 5 shows the validity, reliability, and frequency score TSA determined for each metric and the overall score for each metric subcategory, as detailed in appendix C of its performance metrics plan, dated November 2012. TSA's performance metrics plan defines validity as the ability of the metric to measure BDO performance, reliability as the level of certainty that data are collected precisely with minimal possibility for subjectivity or gaming the system, and frequency as the level of difficulty in collecting the metric and whether the metric is collected at the ideal number of scheduled recurrences.

End Notes

[1] Prior to January 2013, TSA's behavior detection activities, including the SPOT program, were managed by the Behavior Detection and Analysis Division (BDAD). In January 2013, a TSA realignment placed the research and development functions of BDAD within the Office of Security Capabilities, and placed the renamed Behavior Detection and Analysis Program within the Office of Security Operations. As a result of this realignment, TSA now refers to its behavior detection activities, including the SPOT program, as Behavior Detection and Analysis, or BDA.

[2] According to SPOT standard operating procedures, passengers and traveling companions who are referred by BDOs must undergo a standard pat-down, in addition to required passenger screening. The standard pat-downs are generally conducted by transportation security officers, not BDOs.

[3] For the purposes of this chapter, the term "TSA-regulated airport" refers to an airport in the United States operating under a TSA-approved security program in accordance with 49 C.F.R. part 1542 and at which passengers and their property are subject to TSAmandated screening procedures. TSA classifies its regulated airports into one of five security risk categories—X, I, II, III, and IV—based on various factors, such as the total number of takeoffs and landings annually and other special security considerations. Generally, category X airports have the largest number of passenger boardings and category IV airports have the least. The 176 SPOT airports—that is, those airports to which SPOT is presently deployed—include category X, category I, category II, and some category III airports.

[4] Advanced imaging technology screens passengers for metallic and nonmetallic threats including weapons, explosives, and other objects concealed under layers of clothing. At airports participating in TSA's Screening Partnership Program, private companies under contract to TSA are to perform screening functions with TSA supervision and in accordance with TSA standard operating procedures. See 49 U.S.C. § 44920. At these airports, private sector screeners, and not TSA employees, have responsibility for screening passengers and their property, including the behavior detection function.

[5] GAO, *Aviation Security: Efforts to Validate TSA's Screening Behavior Detection Program Underway, but Opportunities Exist to Strengthen Validation and Address Operational Challenges*, GAO-10-763 (Washington, D.C.: May 20, 2010).

[6] Department of Homeland Security, Science and Technology Directorate, *SPOT Referral Report Validation Study Final Report, Volume I: Technical Report, Volume II: Appendices A*

through E, Volume III: Appendixes F through H, and Volume IV: Appendix I SPOT Standard Operating Procedures (Washington, D.C.: Apr. 5, 2011).

[7] HumRRO, *SPOT Validation Study Final Results: 2011 Technical Advisory Committee (TAC) Review Report*, a special report prepared at the request of the Department of Homeland Security, Science and Technology Directorate, June 2011.

[8] Outcome-based performance measures are used to describe the intended result of a program or activity.

[9] GAO-10-763. See also GAO, *Duplication & Cost Savings, GAO's Action Tracker*, Homeland Security/Law Enforcement: TSA's Behavior-Based Screening (Washington, D.C.: April 9, 2013), accessed Apr. 17, 2013, http://www.gao.gov/duplication/action_tracker/1781#t=3.

[10] TISS is a law enforcement database maintained by TSA's Federal Air Marshal Service (FAMS)—TSA's law enforcement agency. The data entered into it may be shared with other federal, state, or local law enforcement agencies. FAMS officials or other law enforcement officials file reports related to the observation of suspicious activities and input this information, as well as incident reports submitted by airline employees and other individuals within the aviation domain, such as BDOs, into TISS. BDOs are to complete a TISS incident report for any situation in which a LEO was involved.

[11] GAO. *Designing Evaluations: 2012 Revision*, GAO-12-208G (Washington, D.C.: Jan. 31, 2012). This chapter addresses the logic of program evaluation design, presents generally accepted statistical principles, and describes different types of evaluations for answering varied questions about program performance, the process of designing evaluation studies, and key issues to consider toward ensuring overall study quality. This chapter is one of a series of papers whose purpose is to provide guides to various aspects of audit and evaluation methodology and indicate where more detailed information is available. It is based on GAO reports and program evaluation literature. To ensure the guide's competence and usefulness, drafts were reviewed by selected GAO, federal and state agency evaluators, and evaluation authors and practitioners from professional consulting firms. This publication supersedes *Government Operations: Designing Evaluations*, GAO/PEMD-10.1.4 (Washington, D.C.: May 1, 1991).

[12] GAO-12-208G.

[13] As required by the E-Government Act of 2002, Pub. L. No. 107-347, § 208, 116 Stat. 2899, 2921-23, agencies that collect, maintain, or disseminate information that is in an identifiable form must conduct a privacy impact assessment that addresses, among other things, the information to be collected, why it is being collected, intended uses of the information, with whom it will be shared, and how it will be secured.

[14] Time charged to other activities, such as SPOT training, leave, baggage screening, or cargo inspection activities was excluded.

[15] We used TSA's May 2012 Current Airports Threat Assessment report, which provides risk rankings of airports based on those that have the highest probability of threat from terrorist attacks.

[16] We randomly selected BDOs from those on duty at the time of our visit.

[17] GAO-12-208G.

[18] DHS, Office of Inspector General, *Transportation Security Administration's Screening of Passengers by Observation Techniques,* OIG-13-91 (Washington, D.C.: May 29, 2013).

[19] Office of Management and Budget (OMB) Circular-A-94, *Memorandum For Heads of the Executive Departments and Establishments on Guidelines and Discount Rates for Benefit Cost Analysis of Federal Programs* (Washington, D.C.: Oct. 29, 1992); GAO, *Streamlining Government: Key Practices from Select Efficiency Initiatives Should Be Shared*

Governmentwide, GAO-11-908 (Washington, D.C.: Sept. 30, 2011); and *Standards for Internal Control in the Federal Government*, GAO/AIMD-00-21.3.1 (Washington, D.C.: Nov. 1, 1999).

[20] We made an effort to interview all 12 TAC members. However, 1 said she attended the meeting but did not participate in the assessment, 1 declined to meet with us because of his position with the President's administration, and 2 did not respond after numerous attempts to contact them.

[21] See Pub. L. No. 107-71, 115 Stat. 597 (2001). For purposes of this chapter, "commercial passenger aircraft" refers to U.S. or foreign-flagged air carriers operating under TSA-approved security programs with regularly scheduled passenger operations to or from a U.S. airport.

[22] The sterile area of an airport is that area defined in the airport security program that provides passengers access to boarding aircraft and to which access is generally controlled through the screening of persons and property. See 49 C.F.R. § 1540.5.

[23] BDOs are not deployed to all TSA-regulated airports, or at all checkpoints in airports where SPOT is deployed. A description of the BDO workforce for the airports included in the scope of this review can be found in appendix IV.

[24] In August 2011, TSA began piloting another behavior detection activity, the Assessor program, during which specially trained BDOs utilized interviewing techniques and behavioral indicators to evaluate all passengers at a checkpoint. In February 2013, BDA officials reported that the pilot had been discontinued, but as of July 2013, officials stated that the agency was reevaluating the Assessor program.

[25] GAO-10-763. We reported in May 2010 that TSA developed the SPOT behavioral indicators, in part, on the basis of unpublished DHS, defense, and intelligence community studies, as well as operational best practices from law enforcement, defense, and the intelligence communities. We also reported that National Research Council officials stated that an agency should be cautious about relying on the results of unpublished research that has not been peer-reviewed, and using unpublished work as a basis for proceeding with a process, method, or program.

[26] BDOs may be deployed outside checkpoint screening areas to perform behavior detection activities as part of other airport security operations, such as passenger screening at boarding gates or undercover plainclothes duty.

[27] TSA, Office of Security Capabilities, *Behavior Analysis Capability (BAC) Risk Based Allocation Methodology: Phase I: Final Report* (Washington, D.C.: December 2012).

[28] BDOs are to attempt to resolve the exhibited behaviors during the casual conversation. BDOs are to continue to watch for behaviors and accumulate any additional behavioral points to the passenger's initial points. If the passenger's cumulative points exceed the LEO point threshold, then the BDOs are to notify a LEO.

[29] TSA, Office of Security Capabilities, *Behavior Analysis Capability (BAC) Risk Based Allocation Methodology: Phase I: Final Report* (Washington, D.C.: December 2012).

[30] TSA has designated "serious prohibited items" from TSA's prohibited items list. See 70 Fed. Reg. 72.930 (Dec. 8, 2005). TSA defines "illegal items" as those items which may be evidence of criminal wrongdoing, such as possession of illegal drugs, child pornography, or money laundering. This chapter hereinafter refers to these items as "serious prohibited or illegal items. LEOs responding to SPOT referrals are officers from local airport law enforcement agencies; federal agencies, such as U.S. Customs and Border Protection, U.S. Immigration and Customs Enforcement, the Federal Bureau of Investigation, and the Drug Enforcement Administration; or other law enforcement agencies. According to SPOT

procedures, BDOs must immediately request a LEO's assistance when any of the following events occur: the individual becomes disorderly, assaults, threatens, intimidates, or otherwise interferes with the screening process; the individual makes a comment about or reference to the presence of an explosive device; the individual refuses to complete screening once the process begins; harm to persons or infrastructure has occurred or is imminent; suspected illegal items are discovered; firearms, weapons, hazardous materials, or explosives are discovered; fraudulent identification or travel documentation is discovered; an artfully concealed prohibited item is discovered; or SPOT behaviors totaling more than a certain point threshold are observed.

[31] The study aimed to answer the following research question: "To what extent does the use of the existing SPOT referral report lead to valid inferences about the traveling population with a focus on high-risk travelers, or persons knowingly and intentionally trying to defeat the security process?"

[32] To select passengers randomly for the validation study, data collection procedures stated that, at designated times, BDOs were to select and observe the first passenger who passed a designated marker at the entrance of a checkpoint screening line. Randomly selected passengers and their companions were to undergo referral screening, without regard to their SPOT scores.

[33] The validation study stated that three reviews of the study were held. The first and second reviews, held in July and October 2010, were focused on making recommendations about additional analyses and future research directions. The final TAC review, in February 2011, involved some participants from the first two reviews and was focused on evaluating the validation study results.

[34] Meta-analyses are reviews that analyze other studies and synthesize their findings, usually through quantitative methods. We reviewed four meta-analyses, which contained analyses of 116, 206, 108, and 206 studies, respectively. Some studies were included in more than one meta-analysis.

[35] Examining verbal strategies used by individuals in interview or interrogation settings has been cited in research as promising in detecting deception because verbal cues are often more diagnostic than nonverbal cues. However, these techniques are not applicable to the SPOT program and are beyond the scope of our work. For example, the SPOT program conducts voluntary informal interviews of passengers—also called casual conversation— after they have been referred for additional screening, not as a basis for selecting passengers for additional screening. Further, since these interviews are voluntary, passengers are under no obligation to respond to the BDOs questions. The nonverbal behavioral indicators included in the studies we reviewed corresponded to SPOT indicators.

[36] M. Hartwig, and C. F. Bond, Jr., "Why Do Lie-Catchers Fail? A Lens Model Meta-Analysis of Human Lie Judgments," *Psychological Bulletin*, vol. 137, no. 4 (2011); C. F. Bond, Jr., and B. M. DePaulo, "Accuracy of Deception Judgments," *Personality and Social Psychology Review*, vol. 10, no. 3 (2006); M. A. Aamodt, and H. Custer, "Who Can Best Catch a Liar? A Meta-Analysis of Individual Differences in Detecting Deception," *The Forensic Examiner*, 15(1) (Spring 2006); and, B. M. DePaulo, J. J. Lindsay, B. E. Malone, L. Mehlenbruck, K. Charlton, and H. Cooper, "Cues to Deception," *Psychological Bulletin*, vol. 129, no. 1 (2003). The first three meta-analyses found, among other things, that the accuracy rate for detecting deception was an average of 54 percent. The fourth meta-analysis found that there were no effect sizes that differed significantly from chance.

[37] Hartwig and Bond, "Why Do Lie-Catchers Fail? A Lens Model Meta-Analysis of Human Lie Judgments." See also A. Vrij, P. Granhag, and S. Porter, "Pitfalls and Opportunities in

Nonverbal and Verbal Lie Detection," *Psychological Science in the Public Interest,* 11(3) (2010). According to this review, the social clumsiness of introverts and the impression of tension, nervousness, or fear that is naturally given off by socially anxious individuals may be interpreted by observers as indicators of deception. Additionally, the review found that errors are also easily made when people of different ethnic backgrounds or cultures interact because behaviors naturally displayed by members of one ethnic group or culture may appear suspicious to members of another ethnic group or culture.

[38] Bond and DePaulo, "Accuracy of Deception Judgments." See also, C. F. Bond, Jr., and B. M. DePaulo, "Individual Differences in Judging Deception: Accuracy and Bias," *Psychological Bulletin*, vol. 134, no. 4 (2008). According to this review, individuals barely differ in their ability to detect deception, that is, poor lie detection accuracy is a robust and general finding that holds true across individuals and professional groups.

[39] S. L. Sporer and B. Schwandt, "Moderators of Nonverbal Indicators of Deception, A Meta-Analytic Synthesis," *Psychology Public Policy, and Law*, vol. 13, no. 1 (2007).

[40] According to TSA officials, in an effort to facilitate sharing of this type of research, as well as validation results and best practices, among countries with behavior detection programs in civil aviation environments, the agency formed a study group together with Switzerland, the United Kingdom, and France. The study group was formed within the European Civil Aviation Conference, an organization of 44 European countries formed to harmonize civil aviation policies and practices and promote understanding on policy matters among its members and other regions of the world. In April 2013, this study group developed a policy paper that established principles of behavior detection in aviation security and discussed some of the practices in programs based in the United States, the United Kingdom, and France. The paper stated that while the programs were similarly based on selecting passengers on the basis of suspicious behaviors, the programs differed in their deployment at airport locations—screening checkpoints, boarding gates, or arrival areas—and used different selection methods—random selection or categorization based on passengers' behaviors.

[41] C. R. Honts, M. Hartwig, S. M. Kleinman, and C. A. Meissner, "Credibility Assessment at Portals." (final report of the Portals Committee to the Defense Academy for Credibility Assessment, U.S. Defense Intelligence Agency, Washington, D.C.: Apr. 17, 2009). A. Vrij, P. Granhag, S. Mann, and S. Leal, "Lying about Flying: The First Experiment to Detect False Intent," *Psychology, Crime & Law*, Vol. 17, Iss. 7, (2011).

[42] P. K. Davis, W. L. Perry, R. A. Brown, D. Yeung, P. Roshan, and P. Voorhies, *Using Behavioral Indicators to Help Detect Potential Violent Acts: A Review of the Science Base.* (Santa Monica, California: RAND Corporation, 2013).

[43] The study discussed factors that affect the use of nonverbal behavior indicators, such as context sensitivity, and individual variability.

[44] As we reported in May 2010, a 2008 report by the National Research Council reported similar findings regarding the connection between behavioral indicators and individual mental states. Specifically, the chapter states that the scientific support for linkages between behavioral and physiological markers and mental state is strongest for elementary states, such as simple emotions; weak for more complex states, such as deception; and nonexistent for highly complex states, such as when individuals hold terrorist intent and beliefs. See GAO-10-768 and National Research Council, *Protecting Individual Privacy in the Struggle Against Terrorists: A Framework for Assessment* (Washington, D.C.: National Academies Press, 2008).

[45] JASON, The MITRE Corporation, S. Keller-McNulty, study leader, *The Quest for Truth: Deception and Intent Detection*, a special report prepared for the U.S. Department of Defense, October 2008. The JASON Program Office is an independent scientific advisory group that provides consulting services to the U.S. government on matters of defense science and technology. Also, Vrij, Granhag, and Porter, in "Pitfalls and Opportunities in Nonverbal and Verbal Lie Detection," state that virtually no research has been conducted on distinguishing between truths and lies about future actions or intentions.

[46] The post hoc fallacy is committed when it is concluded that one event causes another simply because the proposed cause occurred before the proposed effect. For example, the fallacy involves concluding that A causes or caused B because A occurs before B and there is not sufficient evidence to actually warrant such a claim.

[47] For example, see U.S. Naval Research Laboratory, *Behavioral Indicators of Drug Couriers in Airports*, (Washington D.C.: April 2013) and A. Vrij, and P. Granhag, "Eliciting Cues to Deception and Truth: What Matters Are the Questions Asked," *Journal of Applied Research in Memory and Cognition*, 1 (2012) 110-117; and Davis, et.al., (2013). In August 2011, TSA began piloting the Assessor program, during which specially trained BDOs utilized interviewing techniques and behavioral indicators to evaluate all passengers at a checkpoint. In a January 2012 report on the pilot, TSA found that BDOs had difficulty distinguishing between the SPOT and Assessor indicators, which resulted in inconsistent application of indicators. The chapter also found that the ambiguous nature of many of the Assessor indicators "leaves the door open for potential misuse or profiling." According to BDA officials in February 2013, the agency declined to expand the pilot further, in part because it did not fit into TSA's risk-based security strategy. However, in July 2013, BDA officials stated that they were reevaluating the Assessor program.

[48] N. W. Twyman, M. D. Pickard, and M. B. Burns, "Proposing Automated Human Credibility Screening Systems to Augment Forensic Interviews and Fraud Auditing," (paper presented at the Proceedings of the Strategic and Emerging Technologies Workshop at the American Accounting Association Annual Meeting, Washington D.C., Aug. 4, 2012).

[49] In commenting on a draft of this chapter, TSA directed us to several studies related to microfacial expressions. These include M. G. Frank, and J. Stennett, "The Forced-Choice Paradigm and the Perception of Facial Expressions of Emotion" *Journal of Personality and Social Psychology*, vol. 80(1) (January 2001); M. G. Frank, and P. Ekman, "The Ability to Detect Deceit Generalizes Across Different Types of High-Stake Lies," *Journal of Personality and Social Psychology,* vol. 72(6) (June 1997); P. Ekman and M. O'Sullivan, "Who Can Catch a Liar?" *American Psychologist*, vol. 46(9) (September 1991); P. Ekman, W. V. Friesen, M. O'Sullivan, A. Chan, I. Diacoyanni-Tarlatzis, K. Heider, R. Krause, W. A. LeCompte, T. Pitcairn, P. E. Ricci-Bitti, K. Scherer, M. Tomita, and A. Tzavaras, "Universals and Cultural Differences in the Judgments of Facial Expressions of Emotion," *Journal of Personality and Social Psychology*, vol. 53(4) (October 1987). According to the SPOT standard operating procedures, BDOs who have received training on microfacial behaviors are not to use those techniques to assess SPOT behavioral indicator points or to confirm or dispel observations of behaviors.

[50] Other research has also questioned the use of microfacial expressions by security officials to identify potential threats in an airport environment. According to one study, microfacial expressions are more subtle than originally hypothesized and were detected only partially—in either the upper or the lower face but not simultaneously—increasing the difficulty in reliably detecting deceit in a real-time setting. See S. Porter and L. ten Brinke, "Reading

Between the Lies: Identifying Concealed and Falsified Emotions in Universal Facial Expressions," *Psychological Science*, vol. 19, no. 5 (2008).

[51] J. F. Nunamaker Jr., D. C. Derrick, A. C. Elkins, J. K. Burgoon, and M. W. Patton, "Embodied Conversation Agent-Based Kiosk for Automated Interviewing," *Journal of Management Information Systems,* vol. 28, no.1 (Summer 2011). See also American Institutes for Research, "*Behavioral Indicators Related to Deception in Individuals with Hostile Intentions,*" (report prepared for DHS Science and Technology Directorate and U.S. Naval Research Laboratory, Washington, D.C., February 2008).

[52] GAO-10-763.

[53] These outcome measures were developed for the validation study. Possession of fraudulent documents is a subset of possession of serious prohibited or illegal items. According the validation study, the possession of fraudulent documents was studied independently as an outcome measure, since it was the largest class of serious prohibited or illegal items.

[54] Although the SPOT data were potentially unreliable, we replicated the indicator analysis with the full set of SPOT referral data from the validation study to assess the results reported in the validation study, as shown in appendix II.

[55] The 2011 SPOT standard operating procedures lists 94 signs of stress, fear, and deception, or other related indicators that BDOs are to look for, each of which is assigned a certain number of points.

[56] According to TSA officials, given the SPOT operational environment, these methodological constraints were unavoidable.

[57] TSA has contracted for research on the indicators with the same firm that conducted the validation study. The contract, in the amount of $400,000, was to study the effectiveness of the SPOT indicators, among other areas of research. According to the contractor, when designing the validation study, it expressed concerns about how well-defined the SPOT behavioral indicators were and proposed an initial study to work with BDOs to better define behavioral indicators prior to the start of the full validation study. However, TSA moved forward with the field study of the SPOT program without completing the initial study of the behavioral indicators.

[58] The consistency with which two (or more) raters evaluate the same data using the same scoring criteria at a particular time is generally known as inter-rater reliability.

[59] Up to three BDOs may be associated with a referral in the SPOT referral database. According to BDA officials, the BDO in the "team member 1" field is generally the primary BDO responsible for observing the behaviors required for a referral. To avoid double-counting referrals, the referral rate is based on the number of referrals for which a BDO was identified as team member 1. For additional information about the referral rate analysis, see appendix IV and for additional information about our methodology, see appendix III.

[60] We standardized the SPOT referral and arrest data across the 49 airports in our scope to ensure an accurate comparison of referral rates, based on the number of hours each BDO spent performing operational SPOT activities. For a complete description of our methodology, see appendix III.

[61] The average SPOT referral rate across the 2,199 BDOs who conducted SPOT at the airports in our scope was 1.6 referrals per 160 hours worked. Thus, on average, 0.2 percent of a BDO's time, or roughly the equivalent of 1 work day over a 2-year period, was spent engaging passengers during SPOT referral screening. This calculation is based on TSA's estimate that a BDO requires an average of 13 minutes to complete a SPOT referral. The average LEO referral rate for BDOs who conducted SPOT at the airports in our scope was 0.2 per 160 hours worked, or 1 LEO referral every 800 hours (or approximately 20 weeks).

[62] According to TSA officials, there is no minimum referral requirement for any time period.

[63] We conducted a multivariate analysis to examine the associations between the SPOT and LEO referral rates and the specific BDO while controlling for other BDO characteristics. See appendix IV for detailed information.

[64] This is statistically significant at the 0.05 level.

[65] TSA provided monthly aggregate data on some of these variables for calendar year 2012. According to TSA officials, database limitations prevented them from providing earlier data. Our analysis was based on aggregate hourly data for fiscal years 2011 and 2012. As a result, it was not possible to incorporate these additional variables into our analysis.

[66] GAO-10-763. These teams were composed of at least two G-Band, or expert, BDOs, who received an additional week of training on SPOT behavioral indicators and mentoring skills. The teams aimed to monitor airports' compliance with the SPOT standard operating procedures, and to offer assistance in program management, among other things.

[67] These evaluations include a review of BDO compliance with SPOT standard operating procedures, including requirements associated with paperwork and attire.

[68] According to BDA officials, compliance teams will discuss any systematic inconsistent interpretations with airport management, if observed.

[69] These outcomes varied based on the specific outcome measure used to identify high-risk passengers. According to an April 2011 statement before Congress, an S&T official reported that the validation study found that the SPOT program was significantly more effective than a random selection of passengers. Specifically, the official stated that a high-risk passenger was 9 times more likely to be identified using the SPOT program indicators versus a random selection of passengers.

[70] The study's initial sampling plan included 143 of the 166 airports where SPOT was deployed in April 2009. The contractor excluded 23 of the 166 SPOT airports because they were considered small and "non-hub primary" airports (i.e., collectively, publicly owned commercial service airports with less than 0.25 percent of all annual passenger boardings). The 143 airports were grouped into three strata based on the airports' total annual enplanements, and within these strata, on passenger throughput and arrest rates. Further, the contractor made recommendations on the proportion of airports that should be selected from each stratum. The contractor assumed that each airport in each stratum had the same chance of being in the sample as any other.

[71] GAO-12-208G.

[72] One additional airport was added in March 2010, and another 18 airports were added in July 2010.

[73] GAO-12-208G.

[74] According to the validation study protocols, BDOs were to screen randomly selected passengers in the same manner as passengers referred by SPOT procedures.

[75] The remaining four TAC members we interviewed did not comment on this aspect of the study's design.

[76] Validation study training materials state that BDOs were instructed to stop data collection if they observed other passengers exhibiting behaviors that warranted further observation to address airport security concerns.

[77] When LEO arrests are not used, the validation study reported that the SPOT process was slightly more likely to identify passengers with fraudulent documents and serious prohibited or illegal items than random selection.

[78] GAO-12-208G.

[79] According to the validation study, the majority of the arrested passengers were arrested because of possession of a controlled substance.

[80] Outstanding warrants would be discovered by LEOs, who, at their discretion, check the National Crime Information Center to determine if the passenger is wanted by any federal, state, local, or foreign criminal justice agencies or courts. U.S. Customs and Border Protection officials stationed at the airports told us that BDOs may refer passengers who are suspected of possessing fraudulent documents or who are suspected of illegal entry into the United States to make a determination of the passengers' immigration status or validity of immigration documents. TSA officials told us that LEOs may not inform them of the ultimate dispositions of passengers taken into custody, and thus this information may not be included in the SPOT data.

[81] Data collection began in September 2009 at 24 airports during an initial pilot study period and continued throughout the primary study period, which was conducted from December 1, 2009, through October 31, 2010.

[82] Certain details about the findings of the monitoring visits were deleted because TSA considered them to be sensitive.

[83] Study protocols stated that the data collection coordinator was to randomly select passengers by selecting the first passenger to cross a designated selection marker when data collection started. At this airport, the data collection coordinator gave a visual sign to the BDO, who selected the passenger.

[84] GAO-10-763.

[85] TSA, Office of Security Capabilities, *Behavior Detection Officer (BDO) Return on Investment: Final Report* and *Behavior Analysis Capability (BAC) Risk Based Allocation Methodology: Phase I: Final Report*, (Washington, D.C.: December 2012).

[86] TSA's return-on-investment analysis calculated a range of break-even points at which the cost of the BDA program is compared with the calculation of the direct and indirect consequences of a successful attack and the frequency of such an attack.

[87] See, for example, OMB Circular-A-94 and DHS, *National Infrastructure Protection Plan: Partnering to Enhance Protection and Resiliency* (Washington, D.C.: January 2009).

[88] TSA officials told us that the return-on-investment analysis assumed a consequence value on the scale of one September 11, 2001, attack, or $50 billion in direct and indirect consequences, each year. Of the top 12 attack scenarios that the TSSRA identifies for aviation, 4 of the scenarios are on the scale of a September 11, 2001 attack. Additionally, while TSA's analysis explains that changing the attack frequency will change the cost-effectiveness of all security measures, it does not provide any further explanation of how the attack frequency was determined.

[89] Department of Homeland Security, Office of Inspector General. *Transportation Security Administration's Screening of Passengers by Observation Techniques*, OIG-13-91. (Washington, D.C.: May 29, 2013).

[90] TSA's risk-based allocation analysis considered threat, vulnerability, and consequence in a framework to determine where to place behavior detection capability resources nationally to maximize security. TSA's fiscal year 2014 budget request included funding for an additional 72 BDO FTEs beyond its fiscal year 2013 BDO FTE funding levels.

[91] GAO-10-763. Specifically, we recommended that TSA "establish a plan that includes objectives, milestones, and time frames to develop outcome-oriented performance measures to help refine the current methods used by Behavior Detection Officers for identifying individuals who may pose a risk to the aviation system."

[92] See appendix V for a complete list of the performance metrics and their status.

[93] When SPOT was being developed, TSA cited Dr. Paul Ekman, a professor emeritus of psychology at the University of California Medical School, and his work on emotions and their behavior indicators as evidence that behavioral cues can be used to detect deception. However, we reported in May 2010 that after observing the program in practice, Dr. Ekman said research was needed to identify how many BDOs are required to observe a given number of passengers moving at a given rate per day in an airport environment, or the length of time that such observation can be conducted before observation fatigue affects the effectiveness of the personnel. He commented at the time that observation fatigue is a well-known phenomenon among workers whose work involves intense observation, and that it is essential to determine the duration of effective observation and to ensure consistency and reliability among the personnel carrying out the observations.

[94] GAO-11-908. This chapter, among other things, identified key practices associated with efficiency initiatives that can be applied more broadly across the federal government, including reexamining programs and related processes or organizational structures to determine whether they effectively or efficiently achieve the mission.

[95] As discussed earlier in this chapter, LEOs may choose to not respond to a BDO referral.

[96] The LEO referral-to-arrest ratio may be indicative of a relationship between the SPOT behavioral indicators and the arrest outcome measure because an individual must possess a serious prohibited or illegal item, or display multiple SPOT behavioral indicators, for a LEO referral to occur. If the behavioral indicators were indicative of a threat to aviation security, a larger proportion of the individuals referred to a LEO may ultimately be arrested. However, the arrest ratios per airport ranged from 0 to 17 percent.

[97] In a 2012 data audit of the SPOT database, TSA identifies problems with arrest data as one of three categories of "potential errors." However, the audit does not report on the magnitude of this error category, because identifying these errors requires a manual audit of the data at the airport level. In contrast, the audit identifies more than 14,000 potential errors in the other two categories. As a result, we did not have assurance that the arrest data were reliable enough for us to report on details about these arrests.

[98] TSA was unable to provide documentation to support the number of referrals that were forwarded to law enforcement for further investigation for potential ties to terrorism. Further, according to FAMS officials, when referrals in TISS are forwarded to other law enforcement officials for further investigation, the FAMS officials do not necessarily identify why the referral is being forwarded. That is, it would not be possible to identify referrals that were forwarded because of concerns associated with terrorism versus referrals that were forwarded because of other concerns, such as drug smuggling.

[99] During the screening process, the passengers and their traveling companions were found to be in possession of United States currency in amounts ranging from $7,000 to $10,000. SPOT referral reports indicate that these passengers were referred for behaviors. The incident reports stated that passengers were interviewed by LEOs and subsequently released to their flights, and that the chapters of these incidents were forwarded to the U.S. Immigration and Customs Enforcement Bulk Cash Smuggling Center for further investigation. There is no indication on these reports whether the currency was seized.

[100] GAO/AIMD-00-21.3.1.

[101] GAO has identified eight key practice areas for program management of major acquisitions. Although SPOT was not acquired through an acquisition and DHS acquisition directives do not apply, some of the key program management practices could be considered for application in order to mitigate risks and help leaders make informed investment decisions about major security programs. One of these key practices is to demonstrate technology,

design, and manufacturing maturity, the goal being to ensure a program or technology works prior to deployment. Specifically, prior to the start of system development, critical technologies should be demonstrated to work in their intended environment. Likewise, prior to a production decision and deployment, a fully integrated, capable prototype should demonstrate that the system will work as intended in a reliable manner. Given that SPOT's life cycle cost will likely exceed $1 billion, if it were an acquisition, it would be considered a level 1 acquisition, and would be subject to the most rigorous review under DHS's acquisition directives and guidance. Further, these directives require capital asset acquisition programs to undergo successful operational testing prior to deployment and state that the results of operational tests are to be used to evaluate the degree to which a program operates in the real world. See GAO, *Homeland Security: DHS Requires More Disciplined Investment Management to Help Meet Mission Needs*, GAO-12-833 (Washington, D.C.: Sept. 18, 2012). See also DHS's Acquisition Management Directive 102-01 and DHS Instruction Manual 102-01-001.

[102] OMB, *Analytical Perspectives—Budget of the U.S. Government, Fiscal Year 2014.* ISBN 978-0-16-091749-3 (Washington, D.C.: 2013).

[103] We replicated the validation study analysis using the same techniques used by the contractor by (1) creating a series of 2 x 2 contingency tables in which each of the 41 indicators was cross-classified by each outcome, (2) calculating odds ratios to estimate the association between each indicator and outcome, and (3) calculating chi-square values for each table to test the significance of the odds ratio describing the association therein.

[104] The validation study stated that 14 of the 41 SPOT indicators studied were positively and significantly related to one or more of the study outcomes and that the remaining 27 of the 41 indicators did not consistently relate to any outcome. As stated in appendix II, this is inaccurate because our analysis indicates that 20 of the 41 indicators were negatively and significantly related to one or more of the study indicators.

[105] Davis, and others, *Using Behavioral Indicators to Help Detect Potential Violent Acts: A Review of the Science Base*. In its discussion of behavioral indicators, the RAND report includes indicators from "pattern-of-life data"—such as mobile device tracking and monitoring online activity—that can indicate changes in lifestyle patterns, as well as communication patterns and physiological indicators.

[106] For example, the RAND report states that coding emotional expressions for use in scientific studies currently involves a painstaking process of a frame-by-frame analysis in which hours of labor is required to analyze seconds of data, and as such, would be too burdensome to use in real time at checkpoints or other screening areas. The RAND report also states that technologies to recognize and analyze such emotional expressions are in their infancy.

[107] See GAO-12-833. See also DHS's Acquisition Management Directive 102-01 and DHS Instruction Manual 102-01-001.

[108] National Research Council, *Protecting Individual Privacy in the Struggle Against Terrorists: A Framework for Assessment.*

[109] GAO-10-763.

[110] Between August 2012 and October 2012, the OIG interviewed 73 BDOs who were currently or previously assigned to Boston Logan Airport.

[111] See OMB, *Analytical Perspectives—Budget of the U.S. Government, Fiscal Year 2014.* See also, GAO-12-833, DHS's Acquisition Management Directive 102-01, and DHS Instruction Manual 102-01-001.

End Notes for Appendix I

[1] Pursuant to the SPOT standard operating procedures, race, color, religion, national origin, ethnicity, sexual orientation, or disability may be considered if directed by a federal security director, provided such direction is based on specific intelligence threat information.

[2] In its performance metrics plan, TSA recognizes the potential effect of management pressure as it relates to referral rates, and cautions against managers collecting data on the referral rates of individual BDOs because doing so may be misconstrued as a measure of performance, causing BDOs to increase their referrals.

[3] For example, the BDO manager directed BDOs to observe passengers' passports at the travel document checker position for a lack of valid visas or entry stamps and refer passengers without valid visas or entry stamps for screening or directly contact the local law enforcement officer (LEO) or U.S. Customs and Border Protection officer. According to the inquiry report, it has never been the practice of the SPOT program to refer passengers on these criteria.

[4] The OIG reported to us that no formal report was written about the investigation in Honolulu.

[5] According to the DHS memorandum, "[i]t is the policy of DHS to prohibit the consideration of race or ethnicity in [its] daily law enforcement and screening activities in all but the most exceptional instances," as defined in Department of Justice guidance. See United States Department of Justice, Civil Rights Division, *Guidance Regarding the Use of Race by Federal Law Enforcement Agencies* (Washington, D.C.: June 2003). The memorandum continues by explaining that "DHS personnel may use race or ethnicity only when a compelling governmental interest is present, and only in a way narrowly tailored to meet that compelling interest." It further provides that "race- or ethnicity-based information that is specific to particular suspects or incidents, or ongoing criminal activities, schemes or enterprises, may be considered," as stated in Department of Justice guidance.

[6] TISS is a law enforcement database maintained by TSA's FAMS. BDOs are to complete a TISS incident report for any situations in which a LEO was involved. FAMS officials file reports related to the observation of suspicious activities and input this information, as well as incident reports submitted by airline employees and other individuals within the aviation domain, such as BDOs, into TISS. These data are to be shared with other federal, state, or local law enforcement agencies.

[7] The August 2011 SPOT Privacy Impact Assessment Update states that SPOT referral reports do not contain personally identifiable information, but that if a passenger reaches a threshold requiring law enforcement intervention, then personally identifiable information may be collected by a BDO to compare against information in various intelligence or law enforcement databases.

[8] Information collected and entered into TISS may include first, middle, and last names; aliases and nicknames; home and business addresses; employer information; Social Security numbers; other available identification numbers such as driver's license or passport number, date of birth; nationality; age, sex, and race; height and weight; eye color; hair color, style, and length; and facial hair, scars, tattoos, and piercings; clothing (including colors and patterns); and eyewear.

[9] TSA has taken steps to address these issues, including the October 2012 data audit of the SPOT database and has efforts underway to develop a new database that requires a one-time entry of SPOT referral data to populate multiple databases, including TISS. These changes will also create a unique identifier for SPOT referrals to allow officials to easily extract SPOT-related data from TISS. According to a BDA official in August 2013, TSA anticipates that

the development of a new database will begin in December 2013. Further, on an interim basis, TSA has developed guidance designed to help ensure that BDOs enter the SPOT referral number into the body of the corresponding TISS report, which can be identified through a database search.

End Notes for Appendix II

[1] The validation study also stated that the remaining 27 of 41 indicators, or 66 percent, did not consistently relate to any outcome. However, this is inaccurate because our analysis indicates that 20 of the 41 indicators were negatively and significantly related to one or more of the study indicators.

[2] The number of positive and significant associations we detected was slightly larger than the number reported in the validation study largely because we report results from an analysis of the full sample of SPOT referrals, in contrast to the validation study, which used a split-sample approach. In the validation study, a split-sample approach—in which the study data were divided into two stratified random subsets and independent analyses were conducted on each subset—was used, substantially diminishing the power to detect significant associations because the outcome data were sparse or rare events.

[3] Statistically significant at the 0.05 level. Some indicators that were positively and significantly related to one or more outcome measures were negatively and significantly related to other outcome measures. Five of the 41 indicators were unrelated to any of the outcome measures.

End Notes for Appendix III

[1] GAO, *Aviation Security: Efforts to Validate TSA's Screening Behavior Detection Program Underway, but Opportunities Exist to Strengthen Validation and Address Operational Challenges*, GAO-10-763 (Washington, D.C.: May 20, 2010).

[2] DHS, Office of Inspector General, *Transportation Security Administration's Screening of Passengers by Observation Techniques*, OIG-13-91 (Washington, D.C.: May 29, 2013).

[3] The SPOT referral database does not contain any personally identifiable information, such as the passenger's name, home address, or driver's license number.

[4] BDOs are to complete a TISS incident report for any situations in which a LEO was involved. FAMS officials file reports related to the observation of suspicious activities and input this information, as well as incident reports submitted by airline employees and other individuals within the aviation domain, such as BDOs, into TISS. According to the TISS Privacy Impact Assessment, data collected include the passengers' names, home and business addresses, race, nationality, age, eye color, and identification numbers, such as driver's license numbers, Social Security numbers, and passport numbers.

[5] At the time we selected these four airports in mid-2012, both Logan and Detroit airports were participating in Assessor, a pilot program wherein specially trained BDOs perform travel document check screening and interviews with 100 percent of passengers, and refer suspect passengers to checkpoint personnel for additional action.

[6] GAO. *Designing Evaluations: 2012 Revision*, GAO-12-208G (Washington, D.C.: Jan. 31, 2012). This chapter addresses the logic of program evaluation design and generally accepted statistical principles, and describes different types of evaluations for answering varied questions about program performance, the process of designing evaluation studies, and key issues to consider toward ensuring overall study quality. This chapter is one of a series of papers whose purpose is to provide guides to various aspects of audit and evaluation methodology and indicate where more detailed information is available. It is based on GAO reports and program evaluation literature. To ensure the guide's competence and usefulness, drafts were reviewed by selected GAO, federal, and state agency evaluators, and evaluation authors and practitioners from professional consulting firms. This publication supersedes *Government Operations: Designing Evaluations*, GAO/PEMD-10.1.4 (Washington, D.C.: May 1, 1991).

[7] We made an effort to interview all 12 TAC members. However, 1 said she attended the meeting but did not participate in the assessment, 1 declined to meet with us because of his position with the President's administration, and 2 did not respond after numerous attempts to contact them.

[8] GAO, *Assessing the Reliability of Computer Processed Data*, GAO-09-680G (Washington, D.C.: July 1, 2009).

[9] Time charged to other activities, such as leave, baggage screening, or cargo inspection activities was excluded.

[10] We interviewed Charles F. Bond, Jr.; Judee K. Burgoon; Aaron C. Elkins; Pär Anders Granhag; Maria Hartwig; Charles R. Honts; Jay F. Nunamaker; Nathan W. Twyman; and Aldert Vrij.

[11] GAO-12-208G.

[12] GAO-12-208G.

[13] The SPOT referral report contains three fields to enter the names of BDO team members who were involved in the referral. According to TSA officials, the BDO's name entered on the first data field is the BDO who first observed the behavioral indicators and is typically the BDO who is considered responsible for the referral.

[14] At airports participating in TSA's Screening Partnership Program, private companies under contract to TSA perform screening functions with TSA supervision and in accordance with TSA standard operating procedures. See 49 U.S.C. § 44920. At these airports, private sector screeners, and not TSA employees, have responsibility for screening passengers and their property, including the behavior detection function.

[15] GAO-12-208G.

[16] See, for example, DHS, *National Infrastructure Protection Plan: Partnering to Enhance Protection and Resiliency* (Washington, D.C.: 2009); GAO, *Streamlining Government: Key Practices from Select Efficiency Initiatives Should Be Shared Governmentwide*, GAO-11-908 (Washington, D.C.: Sept. 30, 2011); and Office of Management and Budget (OMB) Circular-A-94, *Memorandum For Heads of the Executive Departments and Establishments on Guidelines and Discount Rates for Benefit Cost Analysis of Federal Programs* (Washington, D.C.: Oct. 29, 1992).

[17] This guidance states that estimates that differ from expected values (such as worst-case estimates) may be provided in addition to expected values, but the rationale for such estimates must be clearly presented. For any such estimate, the analysis should identify the nature and magnitude of any bias.

[18] GAO, *Standards for Internal Control in the Federal Government*, GAO/AIMD-00-21.3.1 (Washington, D.C.: Nov. 1, 1999).

[19] As required by the E-Government Act of 2002, Pub. L. No. 107-347, § 208, 116 Stat. 2899, 2921-23, agencies that collect, maintain, or disseminate information that is in an identifiable form must conduct a privacy impact assessment that addresses, among other things, the information to be collected, why it is being collected, intended uses of the information, with whom it will be shared, and how it will be secured.

End Notes for Appendix IV

[1] Pursuant to TSA regulations, a screener must have a high school diploma, a general equivalency diploma, or a combination of education and experience that the TSA has determined to be sufficient for the individual to perform the duties of the position. See 49 C.F.R. § 1544.405(d).

[2] These analyses show the size and significance of regression coefficients, from ordinary least-squares regression models, which reflect the estimated differences in the average number of SPOT referrals and LEO referrals across categories of BDO, and across airports.

In: Behavior Detection Activities ...
Editor: Ronald D. Figueroa

ISBN: 978-1-63117-036-2

Chapter 2

TRANSPORTATION SECURITY ADMINISTRATION'S SCREENING OF PASSENGERS BY OBSERVATION TECHNIQUES*

Department of Homeland Security, Office of Inspector General

May 29 2013

MEMORANDUM FOR: John P. Sanders
Assistant Administrator
Office of Security Capabilities
Transportation Security Administration

FROM: Anne L. Richards
Assistant Inspector General for Audits

SUBJECT: *Transportation Security Administration's Screening of Passengers by Observation Techniques*

---

* This is an edited, reformatted and augmented version of Department of Homeland Security, Office of Inspector General, Publication No. OIG-13-91, dated May 2013.

Attached for your action is our final report, *Transportation Security Administration's Screening of Passengers by Observation Techniques.* We incorporated the formal comments from the Transportation Security Administration in the final report.

The chapter contains six recommendations aimed at improving the Screening of Passengers by Observation Techniques program. Your office concurred with all recommendations. Based on information provided in your response to the draft report, we consider the recommendations resolved and open. Once your office has fully implemented the recommendations, please submit a formal closeout letter to us within 30 days so that we may close the recommendations. The memorandum should be accompanied by evidence of completion of agreed-upon corrective actions and of the disposition of any monetary amounts.

Consistent with our responsibility under the *Inspector General Act*, we are providing copies of our report to appropriate congressional committees with oversight and appropriation responsibility over the Department of Homeland Security. We will post a redacted version of the chapter on our website.

Please call me with any questions, or your staff may contact John E. McCoy II, Deputy Assistant Inspector General for Audits, at (202) 254-4100.

ABBREVIATIONS

BDO	Behavior Detection Officer
DHS	Department of Homeland Security
FY	fiscal year
GAO	Government Accountability Office
LEO	law enforcement officer
OIG	Office of Inspector General
OMB	Office of Management and Budget
PMIS	Performance Measurement Information System
S&T	Science and Technology (Directorate)
SPOT	Screening of Passengers by Observation Techniques
TSA	Transportation Security Administration
TSO	Transportation Security Officer

EXECUTIVE SUMMARY

We audited the Transportation Security Administration's (TSA) Screening of Passengers by Observation Techniques program. The program's intent is to screen passengers by observing their behavior in order to detect potential high-risk travelers. This program uses Behavior Detection Officers to detect passenger behaviors that may be indicative of stress, fear, or deception. Congressman Bennie Thompson requested an audit of TSA's Screening of Passengers by Observation Techniques program to determine its effectiveness, efficiency, and economy as a security screening protocol at airports. The audit objective was to determine whether TSA's Screening of Passengers by Observation Techniques program is structured to ensure that passengers at U.S. airports are screened in an objective and cost-effective manner to identify potential terrorists.

Since the Screening of Passengers by Observation Techniques program began in fiscal year 2007, data provided by TSA indicate that the program has expended an estimated $878 million and has more than 2,800 full-time equivalent positions, as of September 30, 2012. However, TSA has not implemented a strategic plan to ensure the program's success. For example, TSA did not (1) assess the effectiveness of the Screening of Passengers by Observation Techniques program, (2) have a comprehensive training program, (3) ensure outreach to its partners, or (4) have a financial plan. As a result, TSA cannot ensure that passengers at United States airports are screened objectively, show that the program is cost-effective, or reasonably justify the program's expansion. In fiscal year 2012, TSA's Behavior Detection and Analysis Division developed a draft strategic plan that includes a statement of mission, goals, and objectives. However, the plan had not been approved and implemented at the time of our review.

We made six recommendations to improve the effectiveness of the Screening of Passengers by Observation Techniques program. TSA concurred with all recommendations.

BACKGROUND

According to TSA, it conducts passenger and baggage screening for approximately 1.8 million passengers daily at more than 450 TSA-regulated U.S. airports. TSA officials stated that TSA developed and implemented behavior detection as a layer of security (see Figure 1) in response to the *Implementing the Recommendations of the 911 Commission Act of 2007*. The program emphasizes objective behavior observation and analysis techniques to identify potentially high-risk individuals who are engaged in some form of deception and fear discovery.[1] According to TSA, the Passenger Assessment Screening System was based on the behavior assessment concept used by Israeli security forces.

Layers of U.S. Aviation Security

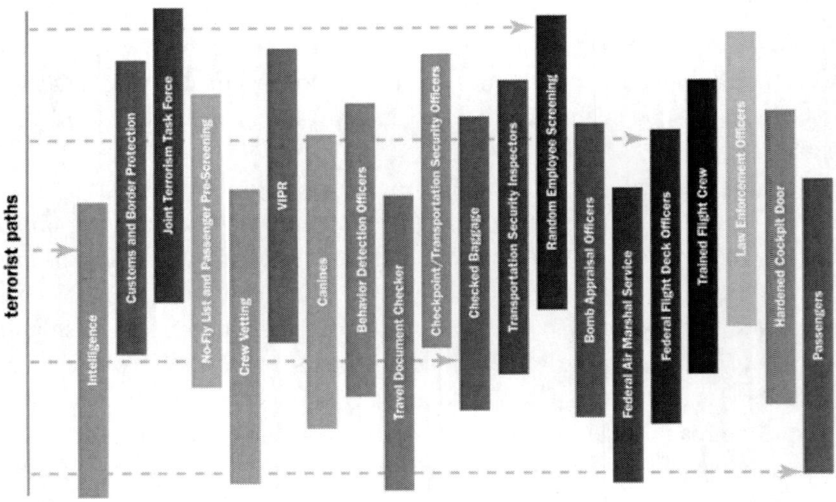

Source: TSA.

Figure 1. Layers of U.S. Aviation Security.

In 2002, Boston's Logan Airport and the Massachusetts State Police/Port Authority piloted the Passenger Assessment Screening System. In 2003, TSA developed the Screening of Passengers by Observation Techniques (SPOT) program with assistance from the Massachusetts State Police. TSA began operational testing at Logan Airport in Boston, Massachusetts, and later expanded its testing at two other New England airports. According to the U.S. Government Accountability Office (GAO), in fiscal year (FY) 2007, TSA implemented SPOT, and was authorized 644 Behavior Detection Officers (BDOs) for deployment to 42 airports. According to TSA, as of FY 2012, more than 3,000 BDOs were authorized for deployment to 176 U.S. airports. TSA's Behavior Detection and Analysis Division is responsible for developing strategic plans and program guidance for the SPOT program.

BDOs, working in pairs, primarily conduct SPOT at airport screening checkpoints by having brief verbal exchanges with passengers waiting in line, while observing passengers' behaviors. A BDO identifies passengers for additional screening based on an evaluation system of identified behaviors, which may require a referral to law enforcement. A law enforcement officer (LEO) may assess the situation by interacting or engaging the passenger to determine if law enforcement intervention is necessary. Passengers whose observed behaviors are not resolved during the referral process may not be permitted to board an aircraft.

TSA BDOs are required to document all relevant information regarding each passenger referral in a referral report and the Performance Measurement Information System (PMIS). However, the SPOT Standard Operating Procedure prohibits the collection of personally identifiable information in the referral report or PMIS. Reports on the results of SPOT operations, such as the *SPOT Situation Report Dashboard – All Airports* are generated from the data entered into PMIS. According to TSA, SPOT referrals made from October 2011 through September 2012 resulted in 199 arrests (shown in Figure 2). The reasons for arrests included outstanding warrants, suspected drugs, and illegal aliens.

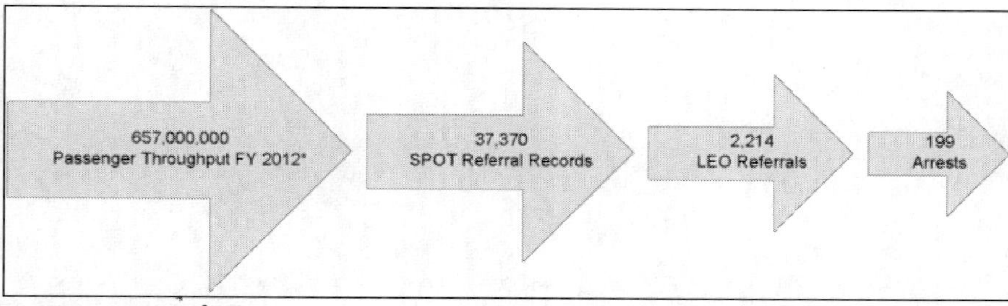

Source: TSA data[2]

* Passenger throughput estimated at more than 450 airports, of which 176 use SPOT.

Figure 2. SPOT Referrals and Arrests, October 2011 through September 2012.

The SPOT program was concentrated at large TSA regulated airports.[3] According to TSA, the insufficient coverage at smaller airports left a gap in TSA's additional layers of security.[4] In FY 2012, the program was expanded to smaller airports to increase the number of passengers potentially screened by BDOs as they enter the air transportation system.

In May 2010, GAO reported deficiencies in the SPOT program and made 11 recommendations; see Appendix B for further details about these recommendations.[5] In addition, the SPOT program has come under scrutiny from Congress and the media. The Honorable Bennie G. Thompson, Ranking Member, Committee on Homeland Security, U.S. House of Representatives, requested that the Office of Inspector General (OIG) conduct an audit of TSA's SPOT program to determine its effectiveness, efficiency, and economy as a security screening protocol at airports.

RESULTS OF AUDIT

Since the SPOT program began in FY 2007, data provided by TSA indicate that the program has expended an estimated $878 million and has more than 2,800 full time equivalent positions as of September 30, 2012. See Figure 3 for data on SPOT program growth. However, TSA has not implemented a strategic plan to ensure the program's success.

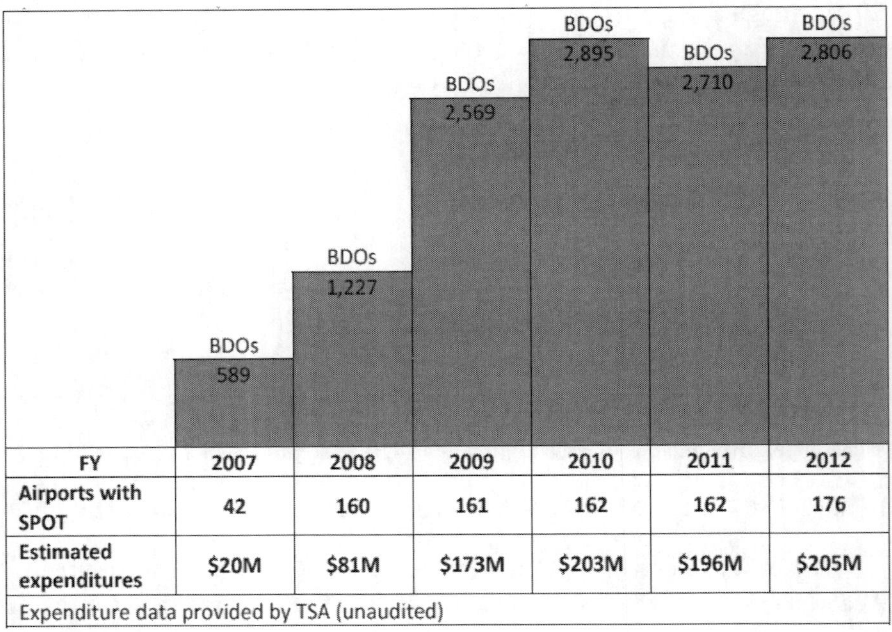

FY	2007	2008	2009	2010	2011	2012
Airports with SPOT	42	160	161	162	162	176
Estimated expenditures	$20M	$81M	$173M	$203M	$196M	$205M
Expenditure data provided by TSA (unaudited)						

Source: OIG analysis of TSA data.

Figure 3. SPOT Program Growth (Estimated expenditures in millions).

An agency's strategic plan is a valuable tool for communicating a common vision to managers, employees, partners, Congress, and the public. Above all, it should be used to align resources and guide decision making to accomplish priorities and improve outcomes. TSA did not (1) assess the effectiveness of the SPOT program, (2) have a comprehensive training program, (3) ensure outreach to its partners, or (4) have a financial plan. As a result, TSA cannot ensure that passengers at U.S. airports are screened objectively, show that the program is cost-effective, or reasonably justify the program's expansion. In FY 2012, TSA's Behavior Detection and Analysis Division developed a draft strategic plan that includes a statement of mission, goals, and objectives. However, the plan had not been approved and implemented at the time of our review.

Performance Management

TSA cannot accurately assess the effectiveness or evaluate the progress of the SPOT program. The program does not have a finalized strategic plan that identifies the mission, goals, and objectives needed to develop a system of performance measures. Even though program operations and referral results are recorded in the PMIS, the referral data captured are incomplete and inaccurate. Unreliable PMIS data cannot be used to measure performance or produce an accurate account of SPOT activity. As a result, TSA cannot demonstrate that BDOs are screening passengers in a uniform manner to identify potentially high-risk individuals. Office of Management and Budget (OMB) Circular A-11 emphasizes that an agency's strategic plan should define its missions, goals, and the means by which it will measure its progress. Specifically, strategic plans should—

- Specify the outcomes that the agency wants to accomplish;
- Ensure that each strategic goal is supported by performance goals or measures; and
- Ensure that performance goals set priorities and targets, and track progress in achieving the goals.

Performance Measures

TSA had not developed performance measures for the SPOT program. The program's Standard Operating Procedure indicates that its purpose is to identify high-risk individuals who may pose a threat to transportation security. The program collects data from referral reports that provide measurable outputs of specific activities. However, these outputs do not provide a measure of program effectiveness, because TSA has not established why these outputs support desired outcomes. For example, TSA documents the identification of prohibited items, undeclared currency, and illegal aliens, but the SPOT program has not defined how these outputs support achieving the SPOT program goals. As a result, TSA cannot assess the SPOT program's success without relative outcome-oriented performance measures. In August 2012, TSA provided its draft *Behavior Detection and Analysis Division Performance Metrics Plan*. This plan is intended to identify current gaps in performance metrics collection, proposed metrics solutions, and resource requirements for the next 3 years. The plan had not been approved and implemented at the time of our review.

Data Collection

Although program operations and outputs from referrals are recorded in the PMIS, the referral data captured are not always complete or accurate. BDO managers are required to review and approve all SPOT referral reports entered into PMIS, but the internal controls over data entry were ineffective. For example, PMIS will automatically bypass manager review of a referral report after 72 hours. There were insufficient data entry quality assurance measures beyond a BDO manager review. Of the 15 airports tested, 1,420 of the 18,152 (8 percent) referral reports recorded in FY 2012 bypassed management review. Five of the airports had more than 15 percent of the referral reports bypass management review. Only 1 of the 15 airports tested had 100 percent management review of referral reports recorded in PMIS.

BDOs are required to document information regarding each referral, including the reason(s) for a referral, the BDOs involved, and the resolution. However, passenger-specific data are prohibited from being recorded.

We assessed more than 110,000 referral records in PMIS from April 1, 2009, through September 30, 2012. Of those records—

- 7,019 did not identify the primary or secondary BDO;
- 1,194 did not meet the criteria for a referral;
- 442 were referral records that were deleted; and
- 143 did not contain a code for the airport where the referral was made.

Additionally, we identified duplicate records and one record that contained personally identifiable information.

Incomplete and inaccurate PMIS SPOT referral data may have been used to present program results to TSA senior leadership and oversight officials to illustrate the results of the SPOT program. For example, 4 months after providing our audit team with PMIS data, the SPOT program office identified and corrected errors in the database before providing similar data to our investigators, who were conducting a separate investigation. We were not informed that the original data we received had been changed. SPOT program officials said they corrected errors in the level of LEO involvement and deleted duplicate records.

Training

TSA has not developed a training strategy that addresses the goals and objectives of the SPOT program. For example, BDO formal training, such as refresher training, is not consistently provided. Additionally, there is no formalized process to evaluate BDO instructors, who provide the only formal classroom training to BDOs, in the Performance Accountability and Standards System. [6] According to GAO, a well-designed training program should be linked to the agency's goals and to the organizational, occupational, and individual skills and competencies needed for the agency to effectively perform.[7] As a result, TSA cannot ensure that training contributes to the uniform screening of passengers.

Formal Training

TSA does not consistently offer formal refresher training to BDOs. Beginning in May 2006, all BDOs were required to attend the SPOT Basic Training course for BDO certification. TSA's training task analysis emphasized the importance of recurring training when it reported:

> ...observation skills are among the perishable variety. They need to be constantly honed and refocused on some regular basis. Observation is the single most important task in the entire SPOT Program....but little training is provided to address its importance, and there is virtually no measurement of the skill in the current testing program.[8]

TSA did not start providing refresher training for currently certified BDOs until May 2011. The 3-day refresher training consists of a review of SPOT Standard Operating Procedure requirements and addresses deficiencies in prior basic training courses. TSA determined that BDOs were not receiving training on 37 of the 63 (approximately 59 percent) required job tasks in the original versions of the basic training course.

BDOs with a year or more of experience are eligible to complete TSA's refresher training. According to TSA, 713 of the approximately 2,200 eligible BDOs (approximately 32 percent) have received refresher training in the past 2 years. Of the 101 BDOs interviewed, 88 were eligible to receive the refresher training. Of the 88 eligible BDOs, 65 (approximately 74 percent) have not received the training. The SPOT program office reported that because of training staffing constraints, they needed to prioritize the training of new BDOs before conducting refresher training. As a result, BDOs who have not received the refresher training may be operating at varying levels of proficiency.

Instructors

BDO instructors provide the only formal classroom training to BDOs. During July 2012, TSA provided training to BDO instructors and tested them on their teaching abilities. TSA identified six BDO instructors who did not have the instructor knowledge, skills, or abilities to instruct BDO classes. TSA provided remedial instruction to those instructors in order for them to become qualified to teach. However, TSA does not evaluate BDO instructors on their instructional abilities in their Performance Accountability and Standards System. Additionally, TSA does not have a program to provide recurrent training to BDO instructors. Therefore, the program office cannot ensure that BDOs are effectively and consistently trained.

Outreach and Engagement

The relationship between BDOs and local LEOs needs to be improved. TSA incorporated law enforcement response as an integral part of the SPOT program. However, the SPOT program office has not ensured that airports effectively engage local law enforcement. BDOs and local LEOs at the airports contacted said that there was insufficient understanding of the roles and responsibilities that each had relative to the SPOT program. For example, LEOs at seven airports contacted said that they had not received clear information about BDO duties and why referrals from BDOs warranted law enforcement response. Conversely, BDOs expressed concerns about the consistency of LEOs' responses to referrals. BDOs said that local LEOs did not consistently respond to referrals or engage referred passengers. TSA data show that LEOs did not respond to approximately 2 percent of the referrals between October 2011 and September 2012.[9] Additionally, TSA data indicate that LEOs did not question approximately 13 percent of referred passengers during that same period.

Of the 15 airports we contacted, 3 had locally developed LEO outreach activities. At the airports using outreach activities. BDOs and LEOs reported more consistent and effective working relationships. The success of the program may be affected if BDOs and LEOs do not collaborate effectively.

Financial Accountability

The SPOT program's financial plan does not include priorities, goals, objectives, or financial performance measures. According to the SPOT program office, the program was allocated more than $1 billion between FYs 2007 and 2012. The data provided by TSA indicate that the program expended an estimated $878 million for the program office and SPOT personnel. OMB Circular A-11 describes budget formulation, development, and execution requirements that include needs analysis and budget development, budget execution, and expenditures tracking. Budget control is an integral part of an entity's planning, implementing, reviewing, and accountability for stewardship of government resources and achieving effective results.[10] Because the SPOT program did not have a financial plan that included priorities, goals, objectives, or measures, TSA cannot (1) show that SPOT was cost-effective, (2) identify opportunities for improvement, or (3) justify the program's expansion.

Prior to FY 2012, the SPOT program office did not fully determine priorities for future spending or develop an itemized forecast of future funding and expenditures. Performance information was not used to assess the effectiveness of program activities to develop budget priorities. According to program officials, the program's historical funding was the basis for spending estimates. Beginning in FY 2012, the Behavior Detection and Analysis Division developed spend plans that identified project funding requirements. According to the FY 2013 draft spend plan, the objective of the spend process is to collect, identify, and document funding requirements for the budget year with a 5-year forecast. However, the spend plans did not include a comprehensive accounting of SPOT funding requirements, such as BDO costs and training.

Resources

BDOs at 12 airports contacted were used for activities not associated with their primary behavior detection duties. For example, nine airports have used BDOs as periodic travel document checkers to review passenger boarding passes and identification at screening checkpoints. The SPOT Standard Operating Procedure allows airports to divert BDOs to travel document checks during times of peak passenger traffic or other urgent circumstances. Additionally, one airport used BDOs to augment travel document checkers in order to identify passengers selected for additional screening. Airport officials explained that they used BDOs because Transportation Security Officer (TSO) travel document checkers were not identifying passengers who needed additional screening. SPOT program officials did not analyze airports' use of BDOs for activities not associated with behavior detection duties to evaluate program performance and financial impact. By diverting BDOs from their behavior detection duties, TSA may be decreasing the effectiveness of a defined layer of security and are not using BDO staff as intended.

BDO Selection, Allocation, and Performance

The SPOT program needs to ensure that it has an effective process to identify and address challenges that may affect the success of the program.

TSA senior airport officials at airports contacted raised concerns regarding selection, allocation, and performance of BDOs. These issues may directly affect the success of the SPOT program. Additionally, TSOs are the only source of candidates for BDO positions. Limiting BDO recruitment may not provide the program with the highest-quality candidates.

TSA officials at the airports contacted said that they did not understand how BDOs are allocated to airports. Federal Security Directors at the airports contacted were unsure whether resources were allocated to airports solely based on the number of passengers boarding planes; or if airport layout, queuing design, and scheduling constraints were also considered. Without a clear understanding of allocation methods and the opportunity to provide input on BDO allocation, TSA officials at airports may find resources limited to the point where the expected benefits of this security layer may not be realized.

TSA does not use an evaluation period to determine whether new BDOs can effectively perform behavior detection and analysis duties. TSA also does not have a process to move BDOs back to their TSO positions without penalty. This may result in a workforce with some BDOs not able to perform their duties effectively.

Conclusion

Strategic planning is the keystone to a successful program. Because OMB Circular A-11 guidance identifies requirements for agency strategic planning, it would be prudent for agency programs to follow these same principles to help ensure program success and contribute to the agency's mission. Without the implementation of a SPOT strategic plan that contains key elements, TSA cannot ensure that passengers at U.S. airports are screened in an objective manner, show that the program is cost-effective, or reasonably justify the program's expansion to ensure that threats to aviation security are effectively prevented.[11]

Recommendations

We recommend that the Assistant Administrator, Office of Security Capabilities:

Recommendation #1:

Develop and implement a comprehensive strategic plan for the SPOT program that includes—

- Mission, goals, objectives, and a system to measure performance;
- A training strategy that addresses the goals and objectives of the SPOT program;
- A plan to identify external partners integral to program success, such as law enforcement agencies, and take steps to ensure that effective relationships are established; and
- A financial plan that includes identification of priorities, goals, objectives, and measures; needs analysis; budget formulation and execution; and expenditure tracking.

Recommendation #2:

Develop and implement controls to ensure completeness, accuracy, authorization, and validity of referral data entered into the Performance Measurement Information System.

Recommendation #3:

Develop and implement a plan that provides recurrent training to BDO instructors and BDOs.

Recommendation #4:

Develop and implement a plan to assess BDO instructor performance in required core competencies on a regular basis.

Recommendation #5:

Monitor and track the use of BDOs for non-SPOT related duties to ensure BDOs are used in a cost-effective manner and in accordance with the mission of the SPOT program.

Recommendation #6:

Develop and implement a process for identifying and addressing issues that may directly affect the success of the SPOT program such as the selection, allocation, and performance of BDOs.

Management Comments and OIG Analysis

TSA provided comments to this draft report. TSA also provided technical comments, which we incorporated as appropriate.

According to its response to the draft report, TSA agreed with our recommendations for improvements to the SPOT program. Below are TSA's responses to each recommendation and our analysis.

TSA Response to Recommendation #1

TSA concurred with the recommendation; however, it disagreed with our assessment that it had not implemented a strategic plan to ensure the SPOT program's success, or that it had not developed performance measures for the program.

According to TSA's response, it is in the process of updating its strategic plan to reflect the organization's recent realignment. The strategic plan will elaborate on the Behavior Detection and Analysis Program's efforts to work with external partners such as law enforcement. Additionally, TSA will execute a BDO training strategy elaborating on many of the efforts that are currently under way. Finally, the Behavior Detection and Analysis Program will continue to produce a yearly spend-plan that identifies goals, objectives, budget formulation and execution, and expenditure tracking.

OIG Analysis

Our report recognizes that TSA had a draft strategic plan and performance metrics plan. However, these documents were not approved or fully implemented at the time of our review.

TSA's planned and current actions are consistent with the intent of the recommendation. This recommendation is resolved, but will remain open until TSA provides its updated strategic plan for our review and has demonstrated progress in implementing the plan.

TSA Response to Recommendation #2

TSA concurred with the recommendation and said that in December 2012, it completed an audit of all SPOT referrals data entered into PMIS between March 2010 and August 2012. Additionally, mandatory guidance was provided to airports in order to correct technical and administrative errors. TSA officials stated that the entire audit and remediation process will be completed by July 2013.

TSA has two information technology initiatives under way to enhance the accuracy and validity of SPOT data. The first initiative, which is scheduled to be implemented in May 2013, will include turning off the ability for SPOT referral reports to automatically bypass manager review after 72 hours. The second initiative creates a new SPOT database that will be more flexible, reduce data entry requirements, and have extensive analytical capabilities. The design and development phases for the new SPOT database will be completed over the next 12 months.

OIG Analysis

TSA's planned and current actions are consistent with the intent of the recommendation. This recommendation is resolved, but will remain open until OIG—

- Analyzes the results of the PMIS data audit;
- Reviews the guidance provided to the airport in order to correct technical and administrative errors; and
- Verifies progress with implementing the information technology initiatives.

TSA Response to Recommendation #3

TSA concurred with the recommendation. According to TSA's response, it has developed and implemented a plan to provide recurrent training for BDO instructors and refresher training for the BDO workforce.

OIG Analysis

TSA's planned and current actions are consistent with the intent of the recommendation. This recommendation is resolved, but will remain open until TSA provides the training plan for the BDO and BDO instructors, and evidence of its implementation.

TSA Response to Recommendation #4

TSA concurred with the recommendation. According to TSA's response, it is going to update its National Training Team Guide for Instructors and Federal Security Directors in May 2013. The update will include a plan to regularly assess BDO instructor performance in core competencies.

OIG Analysis

TSA's planned and current actions are consistent with the intent of the recommendation. This recommendation is resolved, but will remain open until TSA provides the updated National Training Team Guide for Instructors and Federal Security Directors and evidence of its implementation.

TSA Response to Recommendation #5

TSA concurred with the recommendation. According to TSA's response, it is working on two major initiatives to monitor and track the use of BDOs to ensure that they are used in a cost-effective manner and in accordance with the mission of the SPOT program. TSA will begin a nationwide rollout of a BDO Efficiency and Accountability Metrics Database in May 2013.

OIG Analysis

TSA's planned and current actions are consistent with the intent of the recommendation. This recommendation is resolved, but will remain open until TSA provides evidence that the BDO Efficiency and Accountability Metrics Database and Program Compliance Assessment initiatives have been implemented.

TSA Response to Recommendation #6

TSA concurred with the recommendation. According to TSA's response, it has developed and implemented a number of processes for BDOs and BDO managers to provide feedback, suggestions, and concerns to the Behavior Detection and Analysis Program office. Within the next 90 days, TSA plans to capture its communications processes in a BDO Communication Plan, which will include an annual survey.

OIG Analysis

TSA's planned and current actions are consistent with the intent of the recommendation. This recommendation is resolved, but will remain open until TSA provides its BDO Communications Plan and evidence of its implementation.

APPENDIX A: OBJECTIVES, SCOPE, AND METHODOLOGY

The Department of Homeland Security (DHS) Office of Inspector General (OIG) was established by the *Homeland Security Act of 2002* (Public Law 107-296) by amendment to the *Inspector General Act of 1978*. This is one of a series of audit, inspection, and special reports prepared as part of our oversight responsibilities to promote economy, efficiency, and effectiveness within the Department.

The audit objective was to determine whether TSA's SPOT program is structured to ensure that passengers at U.S. airports are screened in an objective and cost-effective manner to identify potential terrorists. Our original audit objective was to determine the extent to which TSA's SPOT program was screening passengers at U.S. airports in an objective and cost-effective manner to identify potential terrorism and/or criminal activity. However, we could not determine the extent to which the SPOT program is operating in an objective and cost-effective manner because the program does not have the necessary structure in place to base our assessment.

To accomplish this objective, we reviewed relevant laws, regulations, and appropriations. We also reviewed program policies, procedures, and other documentation, including versions of a draft SPOT strategic plan, Standard Operating Procedure guidance, and basic training curriculum. We attended the basic SPOT training course given to BDOs to gain an overall understanding of the fundamentals of behavior analysis and how it could be applied. Additionally, we reviewed other agency's audit reports relevant to the SPOT program.

According to OMB Circular No. A-11, *Preparation, Submission, and Execution of the Budget*, July 2010, an agency's strategic plan is a valuable tool for communicating a vision for the future to managers, employees, delivery partners, suppliers, Congress, and the public. We analyzed whether the SPOT program office incorporated the characteristics of an effective strategic plan, including (1) a comprehensive mission statement, (2) general goals and objectives, (3) how goals and objectives are to be achieved, (4) how performance plan goals relate to the general goals and objectives in the strategic plan, (5) external factors that could significantly impact achievement of the general goals and objectives, and (6) a description of the program evaluations used in establishing or revising general goals and objectives, with a schedule for future program evaluations.

We judgmentally selected 15 airports that use the SPOT program (see Table 2). We chose these airports by taking into account the following criteria:

- Number of referrals at each airport for the previous calendar year
- Airport category
- Allocation of BDOs
- Ratios of BDOs, number of passengers boarding planes, and SPOT referrals
- Top 10 high-risk airports from DHS's Current Airports Threat Assessment list
- Physical location (Northeast, Southwest, Central, Pacific Coast)

We interviewed more than 300 officials at U.S. airports, TSA Headquarters, and external agencies. The airport interviews included Federal Security Directors, Assistant Federal Security Directors, BDO program coordinators, BDO managers, BDOs, SPOT instructors, coordination center personnel, and LEOs. Headquarters interviews included program office officials, training division personnel, privacy counsel, SPOT budget officials, database administrators, and allocation and scheduling personnel. In addition, we interviewed officials from DHS' Science and Technology (S&T) Directorate, U.S. Customs and Border Protection, United States Secret Service, and TSA Federal Air Marshal Service. Interviews were also conducted with the Federal Bureau of Investigation and Israel's El Al Airlines security.

We obtained and analyzed the PMIS SPOT referral data for April 2009 through September 2012. We conducted analysis using IDEA Data Analysis Software to assess the accuracy and completeness of referral information collected. Because of insufficient internal controls over PMIS data, we did not rely on the data to form conclusions on performance of the SPOT program.

We obtained and analyzed financial information received from the SPOT program office, including the pay, compensation, and benefit data it sourced from the National Finance Center. We did not test the expenditure data provided by the program office for completeness or accuracy, because financial data for the program from FYs 2007 to 2012 was not readily available.

This audit did not include work to determine the extent to which the SPOT program is based on valid scientific principles for use as an effective layer of aviation security in the United States.

Additionally, on November 9, 2012, TSA announced that it ratified a collective bargaining agreement with the American Federation of Government Employees. The agreement will cover approximately 44,000 TSA employees and took effect on December 9, 2012. Since the audit was concluded in October 2012, the effect of the collective bargaining agreement on the SPOT program was not assessed.

We conducted this performance audit between April and October 2012 pursuant to the *Inspector General Act of 1978*, as amended, and according to generally accepted government auditing standards. Those standards require that we plan and perform the audit to obtain sufficient, appropriate evidence to provide a reasonable basis for our findings and conclusions based upon our audit objectives.

We believe that the evidence obtained provides a reasonable basis for our findings and conclusions based upon our audit objectives.

Table 2. Airport Sample Selection

Airport	Category	BDO Allocation	Referrals from Jan. 2011 to April 2012[12]
Los Angeles International Airport, Los Angeles, CA*	X		3,587
San Francisco International Airport, San Francisco, CA	X		398
Orlando International Airport, Orlando, FL	X		6,981
Tampa International Airport, Tampa, FL	I		1,375
Hartsfield-Jackson Atlanta International Airport, Atlanta, GA	X		601
Chicago Midway International Airport, Chicago, IL	I		440
Chicago O'Hare International Airport, Chicago, IL*	X		730
General Edward Lawrence Logan International Airport, Boston, MA*	X		2,885
Thurgood Marshall, Baltimore/ Washington International Airport, Baltimore, MD*	X		769
Detroit Metropolitan Wayne County Airport, Detroit, MI*	X		1,251
Kansas City International Airport, Kansas City, MO	I		108
John F. Kennedy International Airport, New York, NY*	X		5,293
La Guardia Airport, New York, NY	X		1,618
William P. Hobby Airport, Houston, TX	I		256
George Bush Intercontinental/ Houston Airport, Houston, TX	X		675

Source: OIG analysis of TSA data

*Six of the airports in our sample were on TSA's 2010 list of top 10 high-risk airports.

APPENDIX B: GAO STATUS OF SPOT RECOMMENDATIONS (AS OF 4/10/2013)

(Source: http://www.gao.gov/products/GAO-10-763, GAO official website)

Efforts Validate TSA's Passenger Screening Behavior Detection Program Underway, but Opportunities Exist to Strengthen Validation and Address Operational Challenges, GAO-10-763, May 20, 2010

Recommendation: To help ensure that SPOT is based on valid scientific principles that can be effectively applied in an airport environment, the Secretary of Homeland Security should convene an independent panel of experts to review the methodology of the DHS Science and Technology (S&T) Directorate study on the SPOT program to determine whether the study's methodology is sufficiently comprehensive to validate the SPOT program. This assessment should include appropriate input from other federal agencies with expertise in behavior detection and relevant subject matter experts. **Status**: **Closed – Implemented**

Recommendation: If research determines that the SPOT program has a scientifically validated basis for using behavior detection for counterterrorism purposes in the airport environment, then the TSA Administrator should conduct a comprehensive risk assessment to include threat, vulnerability, and consequence of airports nationwide to determine the effective deployment of SPOT if TSA's ongoing Aviation Modal Risk Assessment lacks this information. **Status: Open**

Recommendation: If research determines that the SPOT program has a scientifically validated basis for using behavior detection for counterterrorism purposes in the airport environment, then the TSA Administrator should perform a cost-benefit analysis of the SPOT program, including a comparison of the SPOT program with other security screening programs, such as random screening, or already existing security measures. **Status: Open**

Recommendation: If research determines that the SPOT program has a scientifically validated basis for using behavior detection for counterterrorism purposes in the airport environment, then the TSA Administrator should revise and implement the SPOT strategic plan by incorporating risk assessment information, identifying cost and resources, linking it to other related TSA strategic documents, describing how SPOT is integrated and implemented with TSA's other layers of aviation security, and providing guidance on how to effectively link the roles, responsibilities, and capabilities of federal, state, and local officials providing program support. **Status: Open**

Recommendation: If research determines that the SPOT program has a scientifically validated basis for using behavior detection for counterterrorism purposes in the airport environment, then the TSA Administrator should study the feasibility of using airport checkpoint-surveillance video recordings of individuals transiting checkpoints who were later charged with or pleaded guilty to terrorism-related offenses to enhance understanding of terrorist behaviors in the airport checkpoint environment. **Status: Closed – Implemented**

Recommendation: Concurrent with the DHS S&T Directorate study of SPOT, and an independent panel assessment of the soundness of the methodology of the S&T study, to ensure the program's effective implementation, and to provide additional assurance that TSA utilizes available resources to support the goals of deterring, detecting, and preventing security threats to the aviation system, the TSA Administrator should provide guidance in the SPOT Standard Operating Procedures or other TSA directive to Behavior Detection Officers (BDOs), or other TSA personnel, on inputting data into the Transportation Information Sharing System and set milestones and a time frame for deploying Transportation Information Sharing System access to SPOT airports so that TSA and intelligence community entities have information from all SPOT Law Enforcement Officer (LEO) referrals readily available to assist in "connecting the dots" and identifying potential terror plots. **Status: Closed – Implemented**

Recommendation: Concurrent with the DHS S&T Directorate study of SPOT, and an independent panel assessment of the soundness of the methodology of the S&T study, to ensure the program's effective implementation, and to provide additional assurance that TSA utilizes available resources to support the goals of deterring, detecting, and preventing security threats to the aviation system, the TSA Administrator should implement the steps called for in the TSA Office of Security Operations Business plan to develop a standardized process for allowing BDOs or other designated airport officials to send information to TSA's Transportation Security Operations Center about passengers whose behavior indicates that they may pose a threat to security, and provide guidance on how designated TSA officials are to receive information back from the Transportation Security Operations Center. **Status: Closed – Implemented**

Recommendation: Concurrent with the DHS S&T Directorate study of SPOT, and an independent panel assessment of the soundness of the methodology of the S&T study, to ensure the program's effective implementation, and to provide additional assurance that TSA utilizes available resources to support the goals of deterring, detecting, and preventing security threats to the aviation system, the TSA Administrator should direct the TSA Transportation Security Operations Center to utilize all of the law enforcement and intelligence databases available to it when running passenger names, for passengers who have risen to the level of a LEO referral. **Status: Closed – Implemented**

Recommendation: Concurrent with the DHS S&T Directorate study of SPOT, and an independent panel assessment of the soundness of the methodology of the S&T study, to ensure the program's effective implementation, and to better measure the effectiveness of the program and evaluate the performance of BDOs, the TSA Administrator should establish a plan that includes objectives, milestones, and time frames to develop outcome-oriented performance measures to help refine the current methods used by Behavior Detection Officers for identifying individuals who may pose a risk to the aviation system. **Status: Closed – Implemented**

Recommendation: Concurrent with the DHS S&T Directorate study of SPOT, and an independent panel assessment of the soundness of the methodology of the S&T study, to ensure the program's effective implementation, and to better measure the effectiveness of the program and evaluate the performance of BDOs, the TSA Administrator should establish controls to help ensure completeness, accuracy, authorization, and validity of data collected during SPOT screening. **Status: Closed – Implemented**

Recommendation: Concurrent with the DHS S&T Directorate study of SPOT, and an independent panel assessment of the soundness of the methodology of the S&T study, to ensure the program's effective implementation, and to help ensure that TSA provides BDOs with the knowledge and skills needed to perform their duties, the TSA Administrator should establish time frames and milestones for its plan to systematically conduct evaluations of the SPOT training program on a periodic basis. **Status: Closed – Implemented**

End Notes

[1] The Screening of Passengers by Observation Techniques Standard Operating Procedure establishes procedures and standards for the uniform screening of individuals.

[2] This information is based on TSA's *SPOT Situation Report Dashboard ' All Airports*, which may be incomplete and inaccurate due to errors identified in the PMIS.

[3] TSA classifies its regulated U.S. airports into one of five categories—X, I, II, III, and IV. Category X airports generally have the largest number of passengers boarding planes and category IV airports have the least.

[4] *Behavior Analysis Capability Risk Based Allocation Methodology Phase I: Draft Report,* July 2012.

[5] U.S. Government Accountability Office, GAO-10-763, *Efforts to Validate TSA's Passenger Screening Behavior Detection Program Underway, but Opportunities Exist To Strengthen Validation and Address Operational Challenges,* May 2010.

[6] The Performance Accountability and Standards System is a pay-for-performance management system that promotes and sustains a culture of high performance and accountability. It is designed to ensure that employees know what they need to do to accomplish their work

successfully and to help TSA accomplish its mission through the use of a pay-for-performance system.

[7] U.S. General Accounting Office, GAO-04-546G, *Human Capital: A Guide for Assessing Strategic Training and Development Efforts in the Federal Government*, March 2004.

[8] Transportation Security Administration, *Training Task Analysis for the Screening of Passengers by Observation Techniques Program*, December 16, 2011.

[9] This information is based on PMIS data, which may be incomplete and inaccurate because of errors identified.

[10] U.S. General Accounting Office, GAO/AIMD-00-21.3.1, *Standards for Internal Control in the Federal Government*, November 1999.

[11] The *Government Performance and Results Act of 1993* requires agencies to develop a strategic plan for program activities that contains (1) a comprehensive mission statement, (2) general goals and objectives, (3) how goals and objectives are to be achieved, (4) how performance plan goals relate to the general goals and objectives in the strategic plan, (5) external factors that could significantly impact achievement of the general goals and objectives, and (6) a description of the program evaluations used in establishing or revising general goals and objectives, with a schedule for future program evaluations.

[12] This information is based on TSA's PMIS, which may be incomplete and inaccurate because of errors identified.

In: Behavior Detection Activities ...
Editor: Ronald D. Figueroa
ISBN: 978-1-63117-036-2

Chapter 3

Statement of John S. Pistole, Administrator, Transportation Security Administration. Hearing on "TSA's SPOT Program and Initial Lessons From the LAX Shooting"*

Good morning Chairman Hudson, Ranking Member Richmond, and other members of the Committee. I appreciate the opportunity to appear before you today to discuss the Transportation Security Administration's (TSA) Behavior Detection and Analysis (BDA) Program.

TSA is a high-performing counterterrorism agency with a dedicated workforce executing our mission around the clock and across the globe. To fulfill this vital mission, TSA employs a layered approach to security through state-of-the-art technologies, intelligence analysis and information sharing, behavior detection techniques, explosives detection canine teams, Federal Air Marshals, and a well-trained frontline workforce, among other assets. All of these layers are essential to securing the nation's transportation systems and improving the experience of the nearly 1.8 million air passengers who fly each day.

While the technological equipment TSA deploys at the checkpoint is designed to detect prohibited items, the BDA program is broader in scope and is designed to detect unknown threats. Terrorists have used a variety of items

* This is an edited, reformatted and augmented version of a statement, presented November 14, 2013 before the House Committee on Homeland Security, Subcommittee on Transportation Security.

to attempt to inflict harm to aircraft, including underwear and shoe bombs, liquid explosives, and toner-cartridge bombs. Consistent across all methods of attack, however, is the malicious intent of the actor. BDOs focus on behavioral indicators, rather than items. Since we cannot always predict the form evolving threats will take, BDOs provide a crucial layer of security. Over the last several years, BDOs have demonstrated that these techniques are an effective means of identifying people engaged in deceptive and/or illegal activity, and those who harbor a fear of discovery, all consistent with behaviors that might appear in individuals planning to do harm on board an aircraft. In 2012 there were 2,116 BDO screening referrals to law enforcement, which resulted in 30 boarding denials, 79 investigations by law enforcement entities, and 183 arrests.

Behavior Detection and Analysis (BDA) Program

The BDA program utilizes non-invasive behavior detection techniques based on scientifically validated behaviors to identify individuals who potentially pose a threat to the nation's transportation network. These individuals are deemed potentially higher risk and subjected to additional scrutiny by TSA. The program was formally established in 2006 after three years of operational pilot testing. Today, TSA deploys more than 3,000 full-time Behavior Detection Officers (BDOs) in the aviation and surface transportation sectors, the latter through participation in Visible Intermodal Prevention and Response (VIPR) teams in surface modes of transportation.

The BDA program identifies potentially high risk individuals exhibiting behavior indicative of excessive fear or stress and re-routes them for additional screening by looking for a combination of individual indicators that warrant follow-up. BDO observations and referrals are not dispositive of high risk activity, but result in additional screening, similar to an Advanced Imaging Technology (AIT) alarm needing to be resolved. BDOs are trained to identify behavior cues that have been shown through research, science, and decades of domestic and international law enforcement experience to be reliable indicators and predictors of anomalous or suspicious behavior. BDOs engage in conversation with individuals displaying anomalous behaviors, looking at possible verbal cues indicative of a high risk passenger and refer those individuals exhibiting such behavior for additional physical screening and/or to law enforcement.

SCIENTIFIC VALIDATION

Behavior detection techniques have been an accepted practice for many years within the law enforcement, customs and border enforcement, defense, and security communities both in the United States and internationally. As a law enforcement professional with 30 years of experience, I can personally attest to the effectiveness of behavior detection principles.

TSA has completed extensive studies in partnership with the Department of Homeland Security (DHS) Science and Technology Directorate (S&T) and the academic community to examine the validity of the BDA program. An S&T validation study in partnership with the American Institutes for Research (AIR) completed in 2011 represents the most thorough and rigorous analysis of a behavioral screening program completed to date. The study included over 70,000 random samples at 41 airports. Notably, the validation study found that TSA's behavior detection identifies high-risk travelers at a significantly higher rate than random screening. The study concludes that a high-risk traveler is nine times more likely to be identified using behavioral detection versus random screening. The 2011 independent Screening of Passengers by Observation Techniques (SPOT) Validation Study Technical Advisory Committee composed of respected subject matter experts from academia, law enforcement, and the intelligence community concurred with the study's main conclusion[1]. Without behavior detection, TSA would have had to randomly subject over 50,000 more travelers to additional invasive screening to achieve the same results as did the BDOs during the timeframe of the two-year study.

INTERNATIONAL BEHAVIOR DETECTION PARTNERSHIPS

TSA has long partnered with international counterparts to develop and strengthen behavior detection practices. In December 2011, TSA partnered with Canada, the European Civil Aviation Conference (ECAC), France, Switzerland, and the United Kingdom to create the Behavior Detection in Aviation Security Study Group (BDIAS-SG) to exchange operational and programmatic information and best practices between/among BDIAS-SG Members in order to refine domestic programs. This framework facilitates the sharing and alignment of ongoing research and science in the field of behavior detection, with a focus on validating the effectiveness and efficiency of behavior detection across cultures and identifying an optimal approach to behavior detection in the future. It also creates international awareness concerning the use of behavior detection as an aviation security measure through the production of non-sensitive outreach materials that clearly define behavior detection. The BDIAS-SG is also creating common tools for use by members and, in the future, regional governmental organizations or possibly industry to support countries/actors with robust security structures to build anomalous behavior detection capability tailored to the relevant domestic environment. This international exchange has been instrumental to the growth and validation of TSA's BDA program and has produced a framework and materials that will assist additional interested countries to establish their own behavior detection programs.

RISK BASED SECURITY

The BDA program is a critical part of TSA's Risk Based Security (RBS) efforts, which moves TSA's checkpoint screening away from a "one size fits all" approach to more effective security measures that use the best available intelligence to differentiate levels of screening based on risk. As concluded in a recent RAND National Defense Research Institute report, "[T]here is current value and unrealized potential for using behavioral indicators as part of a system to detect attacks."[2] TSA behavior detection procedures, including observational assessments and the equally important verbal interaction with passengers, are an essential element in a dynamic, risk-based layered security system.

One key element in expanding RBS is the Managed Inclusion concept, which routes passengers into expedited screening lanes using passenger screening canine teams or sampling with explosives detection technologies to screen passengers and their belongings for explosives while BDOs assess passengers for suspicious behaviors. If the explosives detection teams do not alert on an individual and a BDO does not observe suspicious behavioral indicators, the individual *may* be eligible for expedited screening through a TSA Pre✓TM lane.

ZERO TOLERANCE FOR UNLAWFUL PROFILING

Racial profiling is not part of the TSA's BDA program and is not tolerated by TSA. Not only is racial profiling generally prohibited by Federal law and under Department and agency policy, but it is also an ineffective security tactic. TSA has zero tolerance for this kind of behavior and has taken several steps to reinforce the agency's nondiscrimination and anti-profiling policies with our workforce.

The Standard Operating Procedures (SOPs) and training for TSA's BDA program, in coordination with the DHS Office of Civil Rights and Liberties (CRCL), provide clear instructions to ensure that referrals for additional screening are made based on specific observed behavioral criteria without regard to nationality, race, color, ethnicity, or religious affiliation. BDOs are required to complete a report documenting specific behaviors observed for each passenger identified for additional action. BDA program analysts audit these reports regularly to ensure that BDOs are employing techniques properly, including protecting any privacy information that results from a law enforcement referral.

Additionally, BDOs are trained specifically in preventing race, ethnicity, or religious profiling, and in 2012, TSA reviewed and revised all training documents to underscore that unlawful profiling violates agency policy and anti-discrimination laws. BDOs are instructed to immediately notify management if they believe profiling has occurred. That instruction is reinforced during recurring training, shift briefs, employee counseling sessions, and other avenues. All BDOs and BDO training managers are required to take a pledge against unlawful profiling, and all TSA employees are required to take biannual DHS Notification and Federal Employee Anti-discrimination and Retaliation Act of 2002 (No FEAR Act) training that provides information to employees regarding rights and protections available under Federal antidiscrimination, whistleblower protection and retaliation laws.

TSA expects every member of the workforce, including BDOs, to report allegations of profiling to local management or directly to the TSA Office of Civil Rights and Liberties, Ombudsman and Traveler Engagement (CRL/OTE) or Office of Inspection (OOI) without fear of retaliation. TSA also modified its complaint reporting procedures to make it easier for travelers to report allegations of racial profiling through TSA's website or mobile phone app. If allegations do arise, TSA takes immediate steps to investigate the issue.

In 2013, the DHS Office of Inspector General (OIG) conducted an investigation at the request of TSA into allegations that BDOs at Logan

International Airport (BOS) in Boston, MA, racially profiled passengers in order to meet secondary inspection referral production quotas. In a Report of Investigation provided to TSA on August 22, 2013, DHS OIG stated there was no indication the BDOs at BOS racially profiled passengers.

GOVERNMENT ACCOUNTABILITY OFFICE (GAO) RECOMMENDATIONS

TSA appreciates input and recommendations to enhance its programs including the GAO's feedback on the BDA Program. Its recommendations have led to significant improvements in program management and deployment, including the risk-based allocation mentioned above. In addition, GAO's comments on the behavior indicator set have helped shape TSA's efforts to strengthen detection and evaluation methodologies, including the following actions:

- Condense and strengthen the behavior indicator list and optimize the weights and
- protocols used, which will likely result in significant changes to behavior detection procedures and include a simplified scoring and referral process.
- Explore additional performance metrics that could be used to examine overall program effectiveness, individual and combinations of indicator effectiveness, and reliability across individuals and locations.
- Incorporate more robust data collection and authentication protocols similar to those used in TSA operational tests of screening technologies in any future studies.

While TSA appreciates GAO's partnership in improving the BDA program, we are concerned that its most recent report relies heavily on academic literature regarding the detection of individuals who are lying. The chapter, however, fails to recognize all of the available research or that S&T, which conducted a validation study with an independent review process, relied in part upon unpublished studies not included in literature reviews. It is important to note that TSA's behavior detection approach does not attempt to specifically identify persons engaging in lying; rather, it is designed to identify individuals who may be deemed high-risk based on objective behavioral indicators. The National Research Council's (NRC) 2008 report[3] cites scientific evidence that supports this method.

Based on TSA's objective to identify individuals who may be deemed high-risk based on objective behavioral indicators, TSA believes the program should continue to be funded at current levels while the improvements outlined below are implemented.

FUTURE OF THE PROGRAM

Strong program management is critical to any program and this includes performance metrics, strategic planning, and quality assurance measures. The BDA program is currently undergoing rigorous review to further improve TSA's vital behavior detection capability, which is consistent with many of the OIG recommendations made in their May 2013 report. Within ninety days of the chapter issuance, TSA closed half of the recommendations and is working on closing the remainder. Specifically, TSA has taken the following actions:

- Strategic Planning and Performance Measurement: Finalized a strategic plan and performance measurement plan and began implementing many of the objectives in these framework documents.
- Data Accuracy: Implemented controls to ensure completeness, accuracy, authorization,
- and validity of referral data entered into the Performance Management Information System.
- Training: Implemented a plan to provide mandatory recurrent/refresher training to all BDOs and BDO instructors. In September 2013, The National Training Team Academy, which trains BDO instructors, graduated a class of 25 trainers on September 26. TSA also finalized a plan to assess BDO instructor performance in required core competencies on a regular basis.
- Monitor and Evaluate BDO Activity: Developed and implemented an automated tool to help evaluate airports' use of BDO resources.
- Employee Engagement: Implemented processes, including focus groups, for identifying and addressing issues raised by the workforce that may directly affect the success of the BDA program.

TSA anticipates optimized behavior detection procedures to begin testing by the third quarter of Fiscal Year (FY) 2014 using robust methods similar to the operational testing conducted in support of technology acquisitions. TSA should have sufficient information on the performance of the new processes to update the national behavior detection deployment strategy within six months of the commencement of the tests. Additionally, TSA has established an Optimization effort in partnership with S&T and academia, industry, and other government and community stakeholders to enhance behavior detection principles and provide the tools to quantify its effective contribution to transportation security.

CONCLUSION

The nation continues to face evolving threats to our transportation system, and TSA's BDA Program provides a critical security capability to defend against our adversaries. TSA appreciates the work of the GAO, DHS OIG, and this Committee to identify opportunities to strengthen the program as we move forward. Our ongoing progress demonstrates our continuing commitment to TSA's mission of securing our nation's transportation systems in the most effective way. Thank you for the opportunity to appear before you today. I look forward to answering your questions.

End Notes

[1] SPOT Validation Study Final Results: 2011 Technical Advisory Committee (TAC) Review Report, HumRRO, June 2011.

[2] Davis, P. K., Perry, W. L., Brown, R.A., Yeung, D, Roshan, P., and Voorhies, P. (2013). "Using Behavioral Indicators to Help Detect Potential Violent Acts: A Review of the Science Base". RAND Corporation, National Defense Research Institute.

[3] National Research Council (2008). Protecting individual privacy in the struggle against terrorists: A framework for assessment. National Academies Press, Washington, D.C.

In: Behavior Detection Activities …
Editor: Ronald D. Figueroa
ISBN: 978-1-63117-036-2

Chapter 4

Statement of Charles K. Edwards, Deputy Inspector General, U.S. Department of Homeland Security. Hearing on "TSA's SPOT Program and Initial Lessons from the LAX Shooting"*

Good morning Chairman Hudson, Ranking Member Richmond, and Members of the Subcommittee:

I am Charles Edwards, Deputy Inspector General for the Department of Homeland Security (DHS). Thank you for inviting me to testify today about the Transportation Security Administration's Screening of Passengers by Observation Techniques program, commonly called SPOT. Our audit report, "*Transportation Security Administration's Screening of Passengers by Observations Techniques*" (OIG-13-91, May 2013) concluded that, under the SPOT program TSA cannot ensure that passengers at U.S. airports are screened objectively, show that the program is cost-effective, or reasonably justify the program's expansion.

---

* This is an edited, reformatted and augmented version of a statement, presented November 14, 2013 before the House Committee on Homeland Security, Subcommittee on Transportation Security.

My testimony today will discuss 4 issues in regard to the SPOT program, TSA's: (1) performance management, (2) training strategy, (3) outreach efforts, and (4) financial plan.

In 2003, TSA developed the Screening of Passengers by Observation Techniques (SPOT) program with assistance from the Massachusetts State Police. TSA began operational testing at Logan Airport in Boston, MA, and later expanded its testing at two other New England airports. According to the U.S. Government Accountability Office (GAO), in fiscal year (FY) 2007, TSA implemented SPOT, and was authorized 644 Behavior Detection Officers (BDO) for deployment to 42 airports. According to TSA, as of FY 2012, more than 3,000 BDOs were authorized for deployment to 176 U.S. airports. TSA's Behavior Detection and Analysis Division was responsible for developing strategic plans and program guidance for the SPOT program. The program emphasizes objective behavior observation and analysis techniques to identify potentially high-risk individuals who are engaged in some form of deception and fear discovery. BDOs, working in pairs, primarily conduct SPOT at airport screening checkpoints by having brief verbal exchanges with passengers waiting in line, while observing passengers' behaviors. A BDO identifies passengers for additional screening based on an evaluation system of identified behaviors, which may require a referral to law enforcement. A law enforcement officer (LEO) may assess the situation by interacting or engaging the passenger to determine if law enforcement intervention is necessary. Passengers whose observed behaviors are not resolved during the referral process may not be permitted to board an aircraft.

TSA BDOs were required to document all relevant information regarding each passenger referral in a referral report and the Performance Management Information System (PMIS). However, the SPOT Standard Operating Procedure prohibited the collection of personally identifiable information in the referral report or PMIS. Reports on the results of SPOT operations, such as the *SPOT Situation Report Dashboard – All Airports,* were generated from the data entered into PMIS. According to TSA, SPOT referrals made from October 2011 through September 2012 resulted in 199 arrests, which included outstanding warrants, suspected drugs, and illegal aliens.

AUDIT RESULTS

Since the Screening of Passengers by Observation Techniques program began in FY 2007, TSA data indicate that the program has expanded from $20 million to $205 million in expended costs and the number of airports with the program has grown from 42 to 176. However, TSA has not implemented a strategic plan to ensure the program's success. TSA did not: (1) assess the effectiveness of the program, (2) have a comprehensive training program, (3) ensure outreach to its partners, or (4) have a financial plan. As a result, TSA could not ensure that passengers at United States airports were screened objectively, show that the program was cost-effective, or reasonably justify the program's expansion. In FY 2012, TSA's Behavior Detection and Analysis Division developed a draft strategic plan that included a statement of mission, goals, and objectives. However, the plan had not been approved and implemented at the time of our audit.

PERFORMANCE MEASUREMENT

TSA could not accurately assess or evaluate the progress of the SPOT program because it did not have a finalized strategic plan that identified the mission, goals, and objectives needed to develop a system of performance measures. Furthermore, TSA did not collect accurate or complete information about the program's operations.

The SPOT program's Standard Operating Procedure indicates that its purpose was to identify high-risk individuals who may pose a threat to transportation security, but TSA has not developed performance measures for the program. As a result, the program collected data from referral reports that provided measurable outputs of specific activities; however, these outputs did not provide a measure of program effectiveness, because TSA has not established why these outputs support desired outcomes.

For instance, TSA documented the identification of prohibited items, undeclared currency, and illegal aliens, but the SPOT program has not defined how these outputs support achieving the SPOT program goals. As a result, TSA cannot assess the SPOT program's success without relative outcome-oriented performance measures. In August 2012, TSA provided its draft *Behavior Detection and Analysis Division Performance Metrics Plan*. This plan was intended to identify current gaps in performance metrics collection, proposed metrics solutions, and resource requirements for the next 3 years, but it had not been approved and implemented at the time of our audit.

Although program operations and outputs from referrals were recorded in the PMIS, the referral data captured was not always complete or accurate. BDO managers were required to review and approve all SPOT referral reports entered into PMIS, but the internal controls over data entry were ineffective. For example, PMIS was set up to automatically bypass manager review of a referral report after 72 hours, and the data entry quality assurance measures beyond a BDO manager review are insufficient. Of the 15 airports tested, 1,420 of the 18,152 (8 percent) referral reports recorded in FY 2012 bypassed management review. Five of the airports had more than 15 percent of the referral reports bypass management review. Only 1 of the 15 airports tested had 100 percent management review of referral reports recorded in PMIS.

BDOs were required to document information regarding each referral, including the reason(s) for a referral, the BDOs involved, and the resolution. However, passenger-specific data were prohibited from being recorded.

We assessed more than 110,000 referral records in PMIS from April 1, 2009, through September 30, 2012. Of those records—

- 7,019 did not identify the primary or secondary BDO;
- 1,194 did not meet the criteria for a referral;
- 442 were referral records that were deleted; and
- 143 did not contain a code for the airport where the referral was made.

Additionally, we identified duplicate records and one record that contained personally identifiable information.

Incomplete and inaccurate PMIS SPOT referral data may have been used to present program results to TSA senior leadership and oversight officials to illustrate the results of the SPOT program. In fact, 4 months after providing our audit team with PMIS data, the SPOT program office identified and corrected errors in the database before providing similar data to our investigators, who were conducting a separate investigation. We were not informed that the original data we received had been changed. SPOT program officials said they corrected errors in the level of LEO involvement and deleted duplicate records.

TRAINING

TSA had not developed a training strategy that addresses the goals and objectives of the SPOT program. A well-designed training program should be linked to the agency's goals and to the organizational, occupational, and individual skills and competencies needed for the agency to effectively perform.[1] As a result, TSA cannot ensure that training contributes to the uniform screening of passengers.

Formal Training

TSA did not consistently offer formal refresher training to BDOs. Beginning in May 2006, all BDOs were required to attend the SPOT Basic Training course for BDO certification. TSA's training task analysis emphasized the importance of recurring training when it reported:

> ...observation skills are among the perishable variety. They need to be constantly honed and refocused on some regular basis. Observation is the single most important task in the entire SPOT Program. ... but little training is provided to address its importance, and there is virtually no measurement of the skill in the current testing program.[2]

TSA did not start providing refresher training for currently certified BDOs until May 2011. The 3-day refresher training consisted of a review of SPOT Standard Operating Procedure requirements and addressed deficiencies in prior basic training courses. TSA determined that BDOs were not receiving training on 37 of the 63 (approximately 59 percent) required job tasks in the original versions of the basic training course.

BDOs with a year or more of experience were eligible to complete TSA's refresher training. According to TSA, 713 of the approximately 2,200 eligible BDOs (approximately 32 percent) received refresher training in the past 2 years. Of the 101 BDOs we interviewed, 88 were eligible to receive the refresher training. Of the 88 eligible BDOs, 65 (approximately 74 percent) did not receive the training. The SPOT program office reported that because of training staffing constraints, they needed to prioritize the training of new BDOs before conducting refresher training. As a result, BDOs who have not received the refresher training may be operating at varying levels of proficiency.

Instructors

BDO instructors provided the only formal classroom training to BDOs. During July 2012, TSA provided training to BDO instructors and tested them on their teaching abilities. TSA identified six BDO instructors who did not have the instructor knowledge, skills, or abilities to instruct BDO classes. TSA provided remedial instruction to those instructors in order for them to become qualified to teach. However, TSA did not evaluate BDO instructors on their instructional abilities in their Performance Accountability and Standards System. Additionally, TSA did not have a program to provide recurrent training to BDO instructors. Therefore, the program office could not ensure that BDOs were effectively and consistently trained.

Outreach

The relationship between BDOs and local LEOs is critical to the program and needed to be improved. TSA incorporated law enforcement response as an integral part of the SPOT program. However, the SPOT program office has not ensured that airports effectively engage local law enforcement. BDOs and local LEOs at the airports contacted said there was insufficient understanding of the roles and responsibilities that each had relative to the SPOT program. For example, LEOs at seven airports contacted said they had not received clear information about BDO duties and why referrals from BDOs warranted law enforcement response. Conversely, BDOs expressed concerns about the consistency of LEOs' responses to referrals. BDOs said that local LEOs did not consistently respond to referrals or engage referred passengers. TSA data show that LEOs did not respond to 2 percent of the referrals between October 2011 and September 2012.[3] Additionally, TSA data indicate that LEOs did not question 13 percent of referred passengers during that same period.

Of the 15 airports we contacted, 3 had locally developed LEO outreach activities. At the airports using outreach activities, BDOs and LEOs reported more consistent and effective working relationships. The success of the program may be affected if BDOs and LEOs do not collaborate effectively.

Financial Plan

The SPOT program's financial plan did not include priorities, goals, objectives, or financial performance measures. According to the SPOT program office, the program was allocated more than $1 billion between FYs 2007 and 2012. TSA data indicated that the program expended an estimated $878 million for the program office and SPOT personnel. OMB Circular A-11 describes budget formulation, development, and execution requirements that include needs analysis and budget development, budget execution, and expenditures tracking. Budget control is an integral part of an entity's planning, implementing, reviewing, and accountability for stewardship of government resources and achieving effective results.[4] Because the SPOT program did not have a financial plan that included priorities, goals, objectives, or measures, TSA could not: (1) show that SPOT was cost-effective, (2) identify opportunities for improvement, or (3) justify the program's expansion.

Prior to FY 2012, the SPOT program office did not fully determine priorities for future spending or develop an itemized forecast of future funding and expenditures. Performance information was not used to assess the effectiveness of program activities to develop budget priorities. According to program officials, the program's historical funding was the basis for spending estimates. Beginning in FY 2012, the Behavior Detection and Analysis Division developed spend plans that identified project funding requirements. According to the FY 2013 draft spend plan, the objective of the spend process was to collect, identify, and document funding requirements for the budget year with a 5-year forecast. However, the spend plans did not include a comprehensive accounting of SPOT funding requirements, such as BDO costs and training.

Although TSA had several areas that required improvement, SPOT officials have taken several steps toward meeting those objectives since our audit was issued.

For instance, TSA officials have provided verification that comprehensive measures have been implemented to ensure completeness, accuracy, authorization, and validity of referral data entered into PMIS. They have also developed and implemented a plan to provide recurrent training for Behavior Detection Officer instructors and refresher training for the BDO workforce. Lastly, TSA officials have completed the BDO Communications Plan, which contains a number of workforce engagement tools designed to help the program office gauge selection, allocation, and performance of BDOs.

In closing, strategic planning is the keystone to a successful program. Because OMB Circular A11 guidance identifies requirements for agency strategic planning, it would be prudent for agency programs to follow these same principles to help ensure program success and contribute to the agency's mission. Without the implementation of a SPOT strategic plan that contains key elements, TSA cannot ensure that passengers at U.S. airports are screened in an objective manner, show that the program is cost-effective, or reasonably justify the program's expansion to ensure that threats to aviation security are effectively prevented.

I would also like to take this moment to express my condolences on the tragic shooting incident at Los Angeles International Airport where TSA Officer Gerardo Hernandez was killed and other TSA officials were wounded.

Mr. Chairman, this concludes my prepared remarks. I welcome any questions that you or the Members of the Subcommittee may have.

End Notes

[1] U.S. General Accounting Office, GAO-04-546G, Human Capital: A Guide for Assessing Strategic Training and Development Efforts in the Federal Government, March 2004.

[2] Transportation Security Administration, Training Task Analysis for the Screening of Passengers by Observation Techniques Program, December 16, 2011.

[3] This information is based on PMIS data, which may be incomplete and inaccurate due to errors identified.

[4] U.S. General Accounting Office, GAO/AIMD-00-21.3.1, Standards for Internal Control in the Federal Government, November 1999.

INDEX

A

access, 13, 37, 39, 74, 108
accountability, 97, 109, 125
accounting, 98, 125
acquisitions, 34, 39, 41, 81, 118
adjustment, 59
administrators, 105
African-American, 55, 56
age, 19, 20, 21, 52, 55, 83, 84
agencies, 16, 27, 33, 34, 46, 73, 74, 80, 83, 86, 100, 104, 107, 110
agility, 63, 64
air carriers, 74
alertness, 63
appropriations, 104
arrest(s), 4, 11, 12, 26, 27, 32, 43, 44, 48, 49, 50, 53, 64, 78, 79, 81, 91, 112, 120
assessment, vii, 1, 6, 22, 25, 70, 71, 74, 85, 90, 101, 104, 107, 108, 109, 118
assets, 61, 111
audit, viii, 7, 8, 46, 48, 50, 55, 73, 81, 83, 85, 89, 92, 95, 101, 102, 103, 104, 105, 115, 119, 121, 122, 125
authentication, 39, 116
aviation security, vii, 1, 2, 3, 4, 5, 6, 18, 30, 34, 35, 36, 40, 41, 45, 53, 76, 81, 99, 105, 107, 114, 126
awareness, 42, 63, 114

B

BAC, 3, 74, 80
background information, 45
baggage, 4, 5, 9, 31, 52, 73, 85, 89
bargaining, 105
base, 71, 104
behavioral indicators, vii, 1, 2, 3, 6, 7, 8, 9, 14, 15, 16, 17, 18, 19, 22, 26, 32, 33, 34, 35, 36, 38, 39, 40, 41, 42, 44, 45, 49, 50, 51, 64, 65, 74, 75, 76, 77, 78, 79, 81, 82, 85, 112, 114, 117
behaviors, vii, 4, 9, 10, 15, 16, 17, 18, 22, 25, 39, 43, 44, 46, 54, 65, 74, 75, 76, 77, 78, 79, 81, 89, 91, 107, 112, 114, 115, 120
benefits, 12, 99
bias, 3, 5, 16, 24, 25, 27, 28, 44, 85
BOS, 116
break-even, 80

C

candidates, 99
categorization, 76
certification, 95, 123
challenges, 6, 24, 32, 34, 98
Chicago, 55
child pornography, 74
City, 47

classes, 96, 124
classroom, 95, 96, 123
clothing, 72, 83
clusters, 9
coding, 16, 82
cognitive load, 63
collective bargaining, 105
color, 41, 83, 84, 115
commercial, 9, 25, 74, 79
communication, 43, 63, 82
communication patterns, 82
community(ies), 74, 108, 113, 118
compensation, 105
compliance, 2, 22, 32, 42, 52, 79
composition, 22
Congress, 2, 35, 79, 92, 93, 104
consensus, 40
consulting, 73, 77, 85
contingency, 82
control group, 15
coordination, 104, 115
correlation(s), 14, 16, 18
cost, viii, 2, 12, 29, 34, 35, 53, 80, 82, 89, 93, 97, 99, 100, 102, 103, 107, 119, 121, 125
cost-benefit analysis, 29, 107
counsel, 105
counseling, 115
counterterrorism, 40, 107, 111
covering, 48, 49
criminal activity, 9, 40, 103
cues, 14, 38, 75, 81, 112
culture, 76, 109
currency, 32, 33, 81, 94, 121
curriculum, 104
Customs and Border Protection, 46, 47, 74, 80, 83, 105

D

data collection, 3, 22, 23, 24, 25, 26, 27, 28, 30, 31, 35, 39, 44, 47, 53, 75, 79, 80, 116
database, 7, 17, 32, 43, 46, 48, 50, 54, 73, 78, 79, 81, 83, 84, 95, 101, 105, 122
deficiencies, 32, 91, 96, 123
Department of Defense, 16, 77
Department of Homeland Security, v, viii, 2, 3, 4, 41, 72, 73, 80, 87, 88, 103, 113, 119
Department of Justice, 3, 36, 83
detection, 2, 3, 4, 5, 6, 9, 12, 16, 21, 23, 29, 30, 31, 34, 35, 36, 37, 38, 39, 40, 41, 42, 46, 47, 49, 50, 60, 64, 72, 74, 76, 80, 85, 90, 98, 99, 107, 111, 112, 113, 114, 116, 117, 118
detection techniques, 5, 46, 111, 112, 113
deviation, 28
DHS, 2, 3, 4, 5, 7, 8, 13, 17, 23, 24, 28, 30, 35, 36, 37, 38, 39, 40, 41, 43, 46, 47, 53, 54, 61, 62, 73, 74, 78, 80, 81, 82, 83, 84, 85, 88, 103, 104, 105, 107, 108, 109, 113, 115, 118, 119
directives, 81
directors, 8, 47, 54
disability, 41, 83
disclosure, 8
discrimination, 44, 115
disposition, 88
dissenting opinion, 13
DOJ, 3, 36
draft, viii, 30, 36, 77, 88, 89, 93, 94, 98, 100, 101, 104, 121, 125
Drug Enforcement Administration, 74
drug smuggling, 81
drugs, 32, 74, 91, 120

E

education, 55, 57, 86
E-Government Act, 73, 86
emotion, 16
employees, 72, 73, 83, 84, 85, 93, 104, 105, 109, 115
employment, 52, 56
enforcement, 33, 43, 46, 47, 73, 74, 81, 83, 91, 97, 112, 113, 120, 124
environment(s), 5, 15, 18, 34, 38, 41, 50, 76, 77, 78, 81, 82, 107, 114
equipment, 5, 41, 111
ethnic background, 76

ethnicity, 41, 43, 83, 115
evidence, vii, 1, 2, 3, 6, 7, 9, 16, 25, 30, 34, 35, 36, 40, 41, 42, 45, 49, 50, 54, 55, 74, 77, 81, 88, 102, 103, 105, 117
execution, 97, 100, 101, 125
expenditures, 8, 46, 92, 97, 98, 125
experimental design, 53, 61, 62
expertise, 7, 49, 107
explosives, 62, 72, 75, 111, 112, 114
exposure, 26
external validity, 38

F

fear, vii, 4, 9, 16, 17, 29, 38, 39, 76, 78, 89, 90, 112, 115, 120
federal agency, 9
Federal Bureau of Investigation (FBI), 3, 46, 47, 74, 105
Federal Government, 8, 17, 32, 34, 54, 74, 81, 85, 110, 126
federal law, 47
financial, viii, 8, 46, 89, 93, 97, 98, 100, 105, 120, 121, 124
financial data, 8, 46, 105
financial performance, 97, 124
firearms, 75
flight(s), 11, 81
fluctuations, 52
focus groups, 117
France, 76, 113
funding, 2, 3, 12, 33, 34, 35, 36, 40, 80, 98, 125
funds, 12

G

General Accounting Office (GAO), vii, 1, 2, 3, 10, 20, 24, 28, 33, 53, 58, 72, 73, 74, 76, 78, 79, 80, 81, 82, 84, 85, 88, 90, 91, 95, 106, 109, 110, 116, 118, 120, 126
governments, 49
growth, 92, 114
guidance, 8, 9, 34, 41, 46, 53, 82, 83, 84, 85, 90, 99, 101, 102, 104, 107, 108, 120, 125
guilt, 16
guilty, 107

H

hair, 83
hazardous materials, 75
height, 83
high school, 55, 86
high school diploma, 86
Homeland Security Act, 103
House, 92, 111, 119
House of Representatives, 92
hub, 79
human, 2, 13, 14, 15, 16, 30, 35, 38, 40
human resources, 13

I

ideal, 30, 72
identification, 5, 10, 16, 33, 75, 83, 84, 94, 98, 100, 121
illegal aliens, 91, 94, 120, 121
immigration, 80
Immigration and Customs Enforcement, 47, 74, 81
impact assessment, 7, 48, 54, 73, 83, 84, 86
improvements, 17, 100, 116, 117
incidence, 29
individuals, 9, 14, 15, 16, 38, 39, 46, 73, 75, 76, 80, 81, 83, 84, 90, 93, 94, 107, 109, 112, 116, 117, 120, 121
industry, 114, 118
infancy, 82
inferences, 47, 75
information sharing, 111
information technology, 101, 102
infrastructure, 75
inspections, 52
inspectors, 42
institutions, 49
integrity, 7, 48, 63

intelligence, 46, 74, 83, 108, 111, 113, 114
internal controls, 94, 105, 122
international law, 112
intervention, 66, 83, 91, 120
intoxication, 27
investment, 8, 29, 31, 53, 80, 81
Israel, 105
issues, 14, 48, 49, 73, 83, 85, 98, 100, 117, 120

J

jurisdiction, 47

L

landings, 72
law enforcement, 4, 6, 7, 13, 14, 27, 31, 33, 38, 42, 46, 47, 54, 73, 74, 81, 83, 88, 91, 97, 100, 101, 108, 112, 113, 115, 120, 124
laws, 104, 115
leadership, 95, 122
level of education, 59
life cycle, 82
light, 51
low risk, 37
lying, 15, 39, 116

M

magnitude, 48, 81, 85
majority, 12, 42, 51, 55, 80
management, 11, 34, 41, 60, 70, 71, 79, 81, 83, 94, 109, 115, 116, 117, 120, 122
manufacturing, 82
materials, 25, 46, 47, 54, 79, 114
matter, 2, 7, 36, 40, 41, 49, 107, 113
measurement(s), 66, 96, 123
media, 92
mental state(s), 76
mentoring, 61, 79
meta-analysis, 14, 50, 75
methodology, 5, 7, 8, 13, 18, 47, 50, 53, 73, 78, 85, 107, 108, 109
microexpressions, 16
mission(s), viii, 39, 63, 64, 81, 89, 93, 99, 100, 103, 104, 110, 111, 118, 121, 125
misuse, 42, 77
mobile device, 82
mobile phone, 115
models, 52, 59
modifications, 41
money laundering, 74
motivation, 49
multivariate analysis, 22, 52, 79

N

National Crime Information Center, 80
national origin, 41, 43, 44, 54, 83
National Research Council (NRC), 40, 74, 76, 82, 117, 118
nationality, 42, 83, 84, 115
nervousness, 16, 76
New England, 5, 90, 120
nonverbal cues, 75

O

observed behavior, 10, 29, 91, 115, 120
obstacles, 44
Office of Management and Budget (OMB), 4, 8, 34, 41, 53, 73, 80, 82, 85, 88, 93, 97, 99, 104, 124, 125
Office of the Inspector General, 8
officials, vii, 1, 2, 7, 8, 13, 14, 15, 18, 19, 22, 23, 24, 25, 27, 29, 31, 32, 33, 38, 42, 43, 44, 46, 47, 48, 50, 52, 54, 73, 74, 76, 77, 78, 79, 80, 81, 83, 84, 85, 89, 95, 98, 99, 101, 104, 107, 108, 122, 125, 126
omission, 39
operations, 12, 31, 66, 74, 91, 93, 94, 120, 121
opportunities, 47, 97, 118, 125
optimization, 39, 41
outreach, viii, 89, 93, 97, 114, 120, 121, 124

oversight, 8, 54, 88, 95, 103, 122

P

Pacific, 56, 104
participants, 25, 75
passenger throughput, 51, 79
payroll, 11, 46
PCA, 4
peer review, 38
percentile, 20
performance appraisal, 43
performance measurement, 117
pilot study, 80
police, 38
policy, 22, 43, 76, 83, 115
population, 27, 29, 43, 47, 54, 75
potential benefits, 2, 35
President, 74, 85
principles, 7, 8, 47, 53, 73, 76, 85, 99, 105, 107, 113, 118, 125
prior knowledge, 25
private sector, 72, 85
probability, 51, 53, 73
production quota, 40, 116
professionals, 13
project, 4, 11, 98, 125
protection, 115
prototype, 82
psychological states, 15
psychology, 81
public domain, 38

Q

quality assurance, 94, 117, 122
questioning, 15, 32
questionnaire, 47
quotas, 42

R

race, 7, 20, 21, 41, 43, 44, 46, 52, 54, 55, 57, 83, 84, 115
real time, 16, 38, 82
recognition, 5
recommendations, viii, 6, 13, 29, 31, 46, 49, 75, 79, 88, 89, 91, 100, 116, 117
recurrence, 31, 71
regions of the world, 76
regression, 59, 86
regression model, 86
regulations, 52, 86, 104
regulatory requirements, 9
reliability, 6, 17, 19, 22, 46, 48, 71, 72, 78, 81, 116
religion, 41, 83
remediation, 101
replication, 36
representativeness, 24
requirements, 22, 43, 50, 79, 94, 96, 97, 98, 99, 101, 121, 123, 125
researchers, 5, 13, 15, 16, 49, 52
resolution, 94, 122
resources, 32, 34, 35, 41, 80, 93, 97, 99, 107, 108, 117, 125
response, 5, 18, 29, 30, 39, 43, 45, 88, 90, 97, 100, 101, 102, 103, 124
responsiveness, 22
restrictions, 13
retaliation, 115
rights, 115
risk(s), vii, 1, 2, 3, 4, 5, 7, 8, 9, 12, 15, 17, 23, 25, 26, 27, 29, 30, 31, 32, 34, 35, 37, 40, 45, 50, 53, 61, 64, 65, 66, 72, 73, 75, 77, 79, 80, 89, 90, 93, 94, 104, 106, 107, 109, 112, 113, 114, 116, 117, 120, 121
risk assessment, 29, 107
routes, 112, 114

S

school, 57
science, 15, 40, 77, 112, 114
scope, 8, 22, 29, 34, 48, 51, 74, 75, 78, 111
search terms, 49
Secret Service, 105
Secretary of Homeland Security, 35, 36, 43, 107

security forces, 90
security threats, vii, 1, 6, 7, 35, 45, 49, 50, 108
sensitivity, 63, 76
September 11, 80
services, 77
sex, 43, 83
sexual orientation, 41, 83
shape, 116
signals, 16
signs, 17, 62, 78
Smuggling, 81
Social Security, 83, 84
spending, 98, 125
Spring, 75
staffing, 30, 96, 123
stakeholders, 118
standard deviation, 65
standardization, 22
state(s), 6, 9, 15, 18, 26, 40, 41, 46, 73, 76, 77, 79, 80, 82, 83, 85, 107, 111
statistics, 32
sterile, 9, 11, 74
stimulus, 62
strategic planning, 99, 117, 125
stress, vii, 4, 9, 17, 29, 38, 39, 64, 78, 89, 112
structure, 104
style, 83
subjectivity, 18, 19, 34, 72
suicide, 39
supervision, 72, 85
supervisor(s), 12, 43, 60, 61
suppliers, 104
surveillance, 40, 107
Switzerland, 76, 113

T

tactics, 31
teaching abilities, 96, 124
team members, 63, 85
teams, 2, 22, 31, 32, 79, 111, 112, 114
technical comments, 36, 100
techniques, 9, 14, 15, 16, 36, 39, 40, 74, 75, 77, 82, 90, 112, 115, 120
technology(ies), 5, 14, 16, 30, 34, 39, 41, 72, 77, 81, 82, 114, 116, 118
tension, 76
terrorism, 9, 33, 40, 81, 103, 107
terrorist acts, 39
terrorist attack, 51, 73
terrorist organization, 33
terrorists, viii, 16, 65, 89, 103, 118
testing, 4, 35, 39, 52, 82, 90, 96, 112, 118, 120, 123
testing program, 96, 123
threats, 2, 6, 18, 22, 30, 41, 45, 50, 53, 72, 77, 99, 111, 118, 126
time frame, 22, 34, 80, 108, 109
training, viii, 20, 25, 43, 46, 47, 54, 61, 73, 77, 79, 89, 93, 95, 96, 98, 100, 101, 102, 104, 105, 109, 115, 117, 120, 121, 122, 123, 125
transgression, 16
transportation, 4, 5, 46, 52, 58, 72, 91, 94, 111, 112, 118, 121
transportation security, 4, 5, 46, 52, 58, 72, 94, 118, 121
Transportation Security Administration, v, vii, viii, 2, 4, 21, 41, 60, 67, 73, 80, 84, 87, 88, 89, 110, 111, 119, 126
treatment, 26, 49

U

U.S. Department of Agriculture, 46, 52
uniform, 93, 95, 109, 123
United Kingdom, 76, 113
United States, viii, 1, 5, 9, 27, 33, 72, 76, 80, 81, 83, 89, 105, 113, 121
updating, 101

V

validation, 5, 7, 8, 12, 13, 14, 17, 18, 19, 23, 24, 25, 26, 28, 29, 30, 36, 37, 44, 47, 49,

50, 53, 75, 76, 78, 79, 80, 82, 84, 113, 114, 116
variables, 19, 20, 22, 52, 55, 79
vision, 93, 104
vulnerability, 80, 107

W

Washington, 72, 73, 74, 76, 77, 78, 80, 82, 83, 84, 85, 118
weakness, 25
weapons, 72, 75
workers, 81
workforce, 12, 74, 99, 102, 111, 115, 117, 125
wrongdoing, 74